CANBERRA

Few post-war British aircraft can equal the achievements of the English Electric Canberra. From the moment it appeared, the UK's first jet bomber demonstrated a level of performance deemed scarcely believable from an aeroplane in its class. That helped guarantee one of the industry's greatest sales successes, winning a licence-production contract in the USA — something unheard-of since the First World War. And while the Suez crisis of 1956 provided the RAF's Canberras with their sole front-line action in the bomber role, such was the design's adaptability that a remarkably broad range of other variants fulfilled myriad specialised functions for more than 50 years. Not until 2006 did the RAF phase out its final photo-reconnaissance PR9s, the war in Afghanistan having been their last major operational commitment. To have remained relevant for so long was perhaps the Canberra's crowning glory. And even now, NASA wouldn't be without its highly modified Martin WB-57Fs, very much the ultimate development of the line.

For the type's 75th anniversary year, we are delighted to release this fully updated and much-revised special publication on the Canberra, covering its development and service history, and featuring a stunning range of archive photos. It forms a fitting salute to an aircraft that stole a march on the rest of the world, and reaped the rewards.

Ben Dunnell
Editor, *Aeroplane*

MAIN COVER IMAGE: English Electric Canberra PR.9 G-OMHD displaying at the Farnborough International Airshow in 2014. *(Aviation Visuals/Alamy Stock Photo)*

Contents

CANBERRA

ISBN: 9781802829686
Originally published 2014. Updated 2024
Original editor: Tim McLelland
Updates and corrections: Paul Eden
Senior editor, specials: Roger Mortimer
Email: roger.mortimer@keypublishing.com
Cover design: Steve Donovan
Design updates: SJmagic DESIGN SERVICES, India
Advertising Sales Manager: Sam Clark
Email: sam.clark@keypublishing.com
Tel: 01780 755131
Advertising Production: Debi McGowan
Email: debi.mcgowan@keypublishing.com

SUBSCRIPTION/MAIL ORDER
Key Publishing Ltd, PO Box 300, Stamford,
Lincs, PE9 1NA
Tel: 01780 480404
Subscriptions email: subs@keypublishing.com

Mail Order email: orders@keypublishing.com
Website: www.keypublishing.com/shop

PUBLISHING
Group CEO: Adrian Cox
Published by
Key Publishing Ltd, PO Box 100,
Stamford, Lincs, PE9 1XQ
Tel: 01780 755131
Website: www.keypublishing.com

PRINTING
Precision Colour Printing Ltd, Haldane,
Halesfield 1, Telford, Shropshire. TF7 4QQ

DISTRIBUTION
Seymour Distribution Ltd, 2 Poultry Avenue,
London, EC1A 9PU
Enquiries Line: 02074 294000.

KEY
Publishing

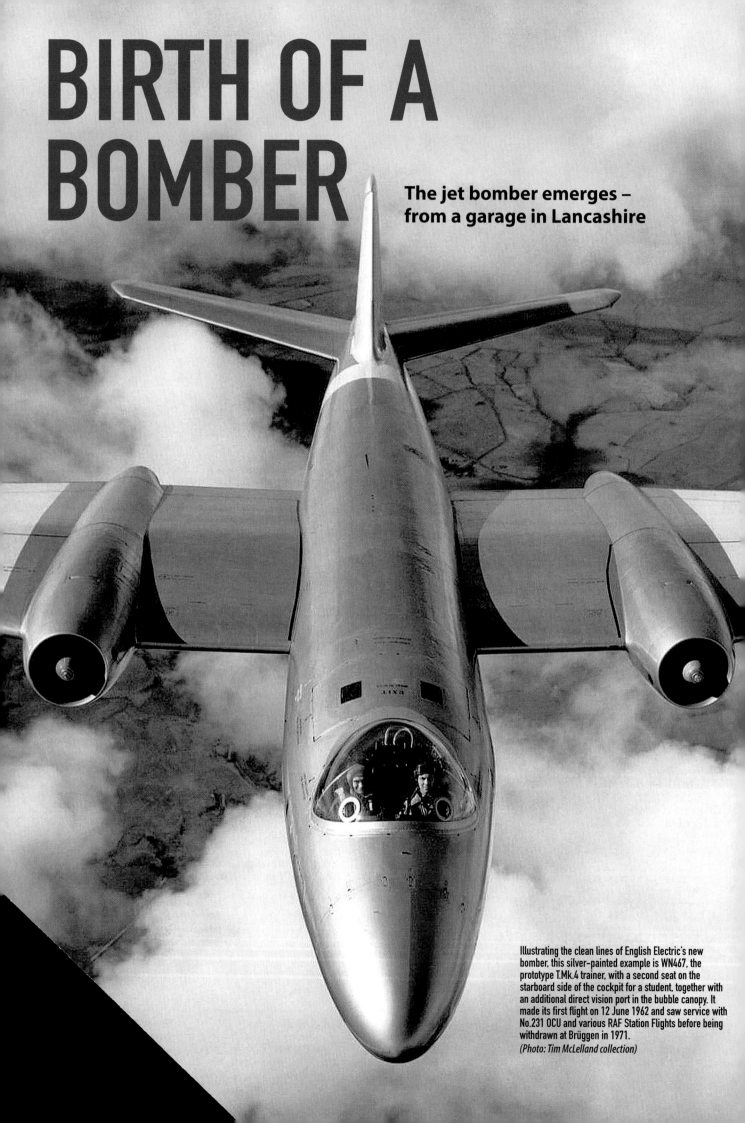

BIRTH OF A BOMBER

**The jet bomber emerges –
from a garage in Lancashire**

Illustrating the clean lines of English Electric's new bomber, this silver-painted example is WN467, the prototype T.Mk.4 trainer, with a second seat on the starboard side of the cockpit for a student, together with an additional direct vision port in the bubble canopy. It made its first flight on 12 June 1962 and saw service with No.231 OCU and various RAF Station Flights before being withdrawn at Brüggen in 1971.
(Photo: Tim McLelland collection)

During the first years of the post-war era, Bomber Command was largely equipped with the Avro Lincoln, a slow and cumbersome machine that was developed directly from the wartime Lancaster. The Lincoln was regarded as an adequate bomber, but it was entirely unsuitable for the 1950s, and the RAF was eagerly awaiting the machine destined to replace it. *(Photo: Aeroplane)*

During the latter years of World War Two, the basic principles of jet propulsion were carefully explored for the first time, and within a remarkably short period, a viable jet engine design was established. The process of developing this knowledge into practical hardware was painfully slow, but the fundamental concept gradually became accepted as a viable proposition, and it was therefore only natural that Britain's aircraft designers would start to consider the ways in which it might be turned into something worthwhile. The British government's Ministry of Supply recognised the potential of the jet engine at a surprisingly early stage and in 1943 (while the Second World War was still in progress) the concept of creating a jet-powered bomber was first discussed at an official level. Although it was impossible to project precisely what might (or might not) be achievable with the new means of propulsion, it seemed likely that jet power would eventually enable military aircraft to deliver greater speeds than would ever be achievable by propeller and piston propulsion, and so it naturally followed that existing aircraft designs might be improved simply by the substitution of jet engines. Whilst this belief certainly held true with respect to potential fighter designs, the same couldn't be said for bombers. It seemed unlikely that the capabilities of the mighty Lancaster could be improved upon by the introduction of a jet-powered derivative (indeed, the earliest demonstrations of jet propulsion produced thrust outputs that were often lower than could be achieved by existing piston engines) because the Lancaster was ultimately built for range and

The United States Air Force supplied a fleet of Boeing B-29s to the RAF from March 1950, as a means of supplementing Bomber Command's strength, and to give Britain an aircraft with far better offensive capabilities than the obsolescent Lincoln. The aircraft (designated as the Washington B.Mk.1 in RAF service) were provided on a lease basis and were returned to the United States early in 1954 after the RAF had begun re-equipping with Canberras. *(Photo: Tim McLelland collection)*

load-carrying capability rather than speed. Therefore, the possibility of giving the Lancaster design a few more miles per hour was barely worth considering. However it did seem reasonable to consider the possibility of creating a new design to replace the Mosquito fighter-bomber, as an aircraft in this category (requiring high speed and manoeuvrability more than range and bomb capacity) would probably benefit most from

the introduction of jet propulsion. Britain's aircraft manufacturers looked at the jet engine's potential with a great deal of interest, but with a war to win it was inevitable that much of their attention was devoted to more immediate concerns, not least the continuing production of existing piston aircraft designs. The idea of a new jet bomber drifted around the stuffy government corridors of Whitehall but

William Edward Willoughby Petter is credited with the conception and preliminary design of the Canberra. Formerly Westland's Technical Director (and designer of the Lysander and Whirlwind), he joined English Electric late in 1944. He steered the Canberra's design and development through its earliest stages but gradually became frustrated by his relationship with the company's directors and left in 1950 to join Folland Aircraft, where he subsequently designed the Gnat trainer. *(Photo: Aeroplane)*

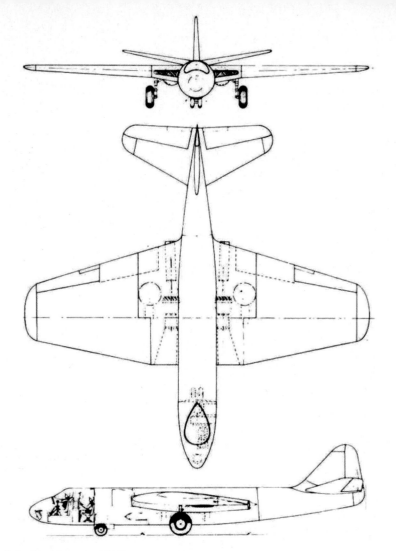

This early drawing of the proposed A.1 illustrates one of the company's first twin-engine layouts, with the two engines positioned adjacent to the fuselage, and main landing gear placed outboard. The subsequent repositioning of the engines was – with hindsight – a questionable step, as it endowed the aircraft with potentially lethal asymmetrical handling qualities at low speed. *(Photo: Tim McLelland collection)*

nobody had enough enthusiasm to do much about it. However, a couple of hundred miles away in Lancashire, the English Electric Company was also investigating the concept of a jet bomber with some enthusiasm. The company had just started to familiarise itself with jet power, thanks to winning an order to produce Vampire fighter aircraft on behalf of de Havilland. Acting as a sub-contractor, English Electric began work on the diminutive jet fighter during 1944 and with a great deal of manufacturing experience already having been gained through the production of Halifax and Hampden bombers for Handley Page, the relatively small company (better-known for the manufacture of tramcars) was beginning to look towards the future.

During July 1944, aircraft designer William 'Teddy' Petter was appointed as the company's new Chief Engineer. Having already earned respect as a designer with Westland, he moved north to Preston with responsibility for overseeing new aircraft design proposals, now that English Electric wanted to expand beyond merely producing aircraft for other companies, and to begin creating its own machines. Within a matter of months a new and highly talented design team had been assembled and while some fairly conventional and unimaginative proposals were investigated, Petter also turned the team's attention to the concept of a jet-powered bomber. But even by the end of 1944 the Air Ministry still didn't truly understand what the jet engine might be able to offer, even though Petter clearly did. Back in 1944 the idea of abandoning propellers in favour of noisy tubes of hot air seemed to be more of an abstract scientific concept than a serious military possibility. But

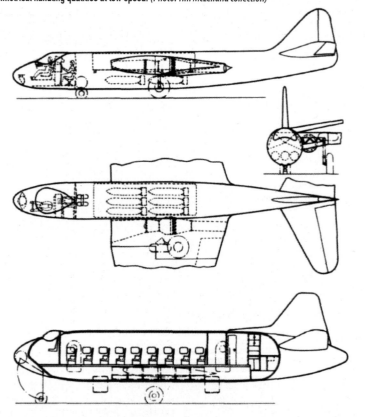

In addition to creating a variety of initial bomber designs for the A.1, the company also considered the possibility of creating a 34-passenger airliner, using the same wings and tail structure, although the project never progressed beyond the concept stage. *(Photo: Tim McLelland collection)*

⤊ English Electric acquired the former USAAF airfield at Warton in 1946 in order to expand its manufacturing facilities that were concentrated at nearby Samlesbury. Most of the Canberra's design and initial construction work took place here, as was all test flying. The site was gradually developed and has continued to expand until the present day. It is now the manufacturing base for the RAF's Typhoon fleet as part of BAE Systems. *(Photo: Tim McLelland collection)*

(Top left) This unremarkable bus garage in Preston's Corporation Street was the site where the Canberra was conceived. Petter's design team was based in offices here during the early days of the A.1 project until facilities were prepared at Warton. *(Photo: Tim McLelland collection)*

⤙ Modern military aircraft are inevitably rolled out with fanfare and ceremony but the A.1 emerged from its hangar without fuss. Engine testing was performed out on the airfield prior to taxi trials and short, high-speed "hops" to evaluate the aircraft's control responses.
(Photo: Tim McLelland collection)

A significant moment in aviation history as the prototype English Electric A.1 (VN999) reaches the end of its assembly at Warton, early in 1949. *(Photo: Tim McLelland collection)* ➤

▲◄ These Air Ministry photographs were taken shortly before the A.1's first flight on 13 May 1949. Very few photographs of the A.1 were released to the media and it wasn't until the SBAC show at Farnborough in September that the public got its first proper look at the new bomber.
Photos: Tim McLelland collection)

▼ Engine testing was performed at Warton during the first weeks of May 1949. As can be seen, the Avon's engine cowlings are removed, enabling engineers to access components swiftly. Of particular note is the rounded rudder tip and dorsal fairing ahead of the fin. These were soon redesigned following the initial test flights. *(Photo: Aeroplane)*

▼ A rare photograph of VN799 during an engine test run at Warton, shortly before the aircraft's maiden flight in March 1949. The large, rounded fin is clearly visible, and a sliver of daylight is visible under the tailplane, illustrating the one-piece adjustable structure in nose-up trim. *(Photo: Tim McLelland collection)*

English Electric took a rather different view. The company's active interest in the subject (and continual communications with the Air Ministry) finally had some direct effect, and the Air Staff finally began to accept that there was a good case for developing some sort of jet design. Although English Electric initially looked at ways to produce a successor to the Mosquito, the Air Ministry expressed its interest in something rather more ambitious that was finally expressed as a "high-altitude and high-speed bomber" powered by turbojet engines. Neither a Mosquito nor a Lancaster, the jet bomber would be something in between. This interest in a bigger and more substantial machine was probably due to a number of factors. First, it was becoming increasingly evident that the

Lancaster would soon be obsolete and its successor (the Lincoln) was hardly any better. Therefore, a completely new bomber design would be necessary, be it jet-powered or otherwise. Likewise, the development of atomic weapons was still a carefully guarded secret but it was a vitally important issue that was gradually becoming known to more officials within the Air Ministry. Consequently, the new technology almost certainly had an influence on the developing interest in a new jet bomber, even though the new aircraft was not (at least overtly) designed with atomic warfare in mind.

The Ministry of Supply issued Specification E.3/45 based around the basic concept of a new high-speed bomber, and Petter's team embarked on a company

project to meet this specification, designated as the A.1 by English Electric. The ministry's main specification called for a 'high-speed and high-altitude unarmed bomber' with a nominal cruising speed of 500kts at 40,000ft and a ceiling of 50,000ft. It was envisaged that only a two-man crew would be needed, comprising a pilot and a navigator who would also be responsible for additional tasks such as radio and radar operation. A radar bombing system was considered appropriate rather than old-fashioned visual bombing: "The aircraft is to be laid out for bomb aiming by radar and other mechanical vision systems and for the use of guided projectiles". The stipulation that the aircraft should be without defensive armament was an indication of the Air Staff's belief that if it had sufficient speed, ➤

altitude and agility, it would not need to be fettered by heavy and cumbersome guns in order to defend itself. This was perhaps an ambitious and unrealistic expectation in 1945 but the Air Staff's optimistic attitude was eventually justified.

English Electric created a design that met the necessary requirements (or at least showed the promise of doing so) and submitted a brochure to the Ministry of Supply in September 1945. The proposed design was the culmination of a great deal of thinking that had originated in Somerset when Petter was still with Westland Aircraft. At that time he had considered the possibility of creating a relatively small aircraft powered by Metropolitan-Vickers Beryl turbojets (an engine that was eventually developed into the Sapphire). That idea was never pursued but when the Air Ministry began shifting its interest towards a more conventional high-altitude bombing platform, the Beryl engine seemed inadequate for the task. Rolls-Royce was developing a new 12,500lb thrust engine, and although its centrifugal-flow system (the type of engine used in the Gloster Meteor) would result in a pretty bulky piece of equipment, it could still be accommodated within a large circular fuselage structure. Thus, Petter and his team drew up some design concepts that suited this arrangement, with a simple tubular fuselage of 6ft 6in diameter. However the Rolls-Royce engine didn't proceed very far, not least because the company was achieving great success with its new axial-flow AJ.65 engine, and this was capable of delivering 6,000lb of thrust even without all the weight and complications of the clumsy centrifugal system. It didn't need much imagination to realise that two of the smaller and much slimmer AJ.65 engines would be a far better solution, not only because they would be small enough to be housed either inside or under the wings, but because the aircraft would also have a degree of additional safety should one engine fail (early jet engines were notoriously unreliable).

Dr. A.A. Griffith at Rolls-Royce recommended that axial-flow turbojets would be the logical way forward and English Electric dropped its original proposal in favour of a much more refined design incorporating two engines, each buried in the wing root structure (hiding engines in the wing to reduce airflow drag was a new innovation that many British designers embraced at this time). The new design naturally offered better fuel consumption figures, and this enabled the designers to reduce the aircraft's fuel tankage, and enlarge the bomb bay, so that a very respectable weapons load could be carried. It was predicted that the relatively conservative wing design (essentially straight with a slightly swept leading edge) would enable the bomber to fly at speeds up to 550mph, although the use of a swept wing would have probably increased this figure to 585mph. However Petter didn't see any advantage in aiming for this higher speed if it meant long

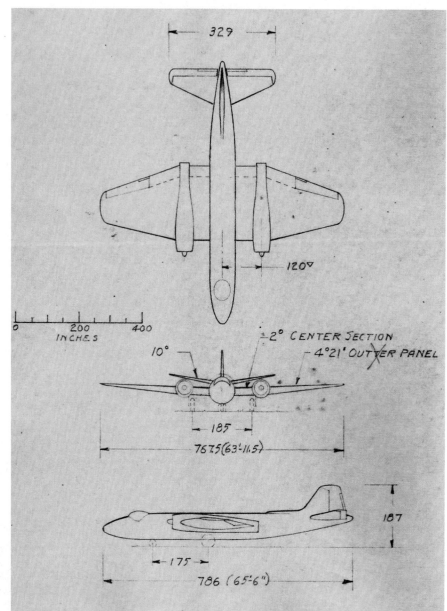

High above the Lancashire countryside, English Electric's A.1 in the hands of test pilot Roland Beamont.
(Photos: Aeroplane)

delays and rises in cost, both of which would be inevitable if a swept-wing design was pursued. The concept of swept wings was very new in 1945 and even though the scientific data (mostly captured from Nazi Germany) indicated that the idea was sound, it was a radical concept that seemed likely to require a great deal of time-consuming - and expensive - testing. Instead, it was agreed from the outset that a more predictable and conventional straight-wing design should be adopted, and the two engines should be moved outwards from the wing root so that a wide track landing gear could be fitted, enabling the main wheels to retract neatly into the deep inner wing structure. The decision to shift the engines outboard made sense, but the new position meant that streamlined nacelles had to be incorporated

into the wing structure, and that the almost drag-free advantages of a fully buried engine were lost. More significantly, the new engine position saw to it that the aircraft would have far less asymmetrical stability should either engine fail. This didn't seem to be much of a concern at the time but it was something that eventually became a significant flaw when the aircraft finally entered service with the RAF. Despite this, the new wing design was fixed and the earlier design's conventional tail and fin structure was retained, creating a simple but surprisingly elegant aircraft that the Air Ministry and Ministry of Supply welcomed with great excitement.

The first production contract was issued to English Electric on 7 January 1946, calling for a fleet of four prototypes. A wooden

mock-up was constructed so that the basic construction procedure could be explored and established before production of the actual aircraft got underway. Significantly, English Electric abandoned 'hand building' techniques and introduced production jigs, ensuring that each of the major components would be identical, so that primary structures were interchangeable between aircraft. The key structures were the front, centre and rear fuselage sections, the mainplanes (wings) for the early aircraft (which were not fitted with deicing systems) and later mainplanes for a development-standard engine and anti-icing gear. This production technique was relatively new at the time but it proved invaluable for the company in later years when the same aircraft was produced in many different versions, and components

VN799 at Warton a few weeks after its first flight, by which stage the large, rounded rudder had been replaced by a smaller square-edged structure, although the dorsal fillet ahead of the fin leading edge is still attached. This was subsequently removed as it had only a negligible effect on the aircraft's performance. Also visible is the original canopy layout. This was modified with a metal cowling attached to the rear portion, designed to eradicate turbulence in that area.
(Photo: Tim McLelland collection)

The photograph on the left of the prototype Canberra PR.Mk.3 provides an interesting contrast with the previous image, having been taken at the same location. It shows the later production–standard tail structure, the modified cockpit canopy, and the clear nose section that was designed to enable visual bomb aiming to be performed. Less noticeable is the fuselage extension ahead of the wing leading edge, designed to provide additional capacity for camera equipment. *(Photo: Tim McLelland collection)*

The A.1 prototype arriving at the 1949 Farnborough SBAC show. Pictured just seconds from touchdown as it passes over Farnborough's famous Black Sheds. *(Photo: Aeroplane)*

were interchanged in order to equip the aeroplanes for specific roles or to replace sections that were either damaged or fatigued. The Rolls-Royce AJ.65 became the preferred powerplant for the aircraft but, as English Electric had feared, development and production schedules for the engine (the Avon) began to slip and in order to avoid delaying test flights of the new A.1 bomber, a pair of 5,000lb Nene engines was allocated to what eventually became the second prototype, these centrifugal-flow units requiring fatter, re-contoured nacelles in order to accommodate their greater bulk. This wasn't an ideal solution to the engine delays, but it ensured that the bomber could begin flight development without delay, while Rolls-Royce continued to work on the Avon. However, the worries over production of the AJ.65 were soon resolved and the

Nene-powered second prototype eventually became little more than a rather expensive precautionary diversion that was ultimately unnecessary. The first prototype was VN799, which was slowly completed at the company's Strand Road factory before being dismantled for transportation to nearby Warton, a former US Army Air Forces (USAAF) airfield adjacent to the Ribble estuary that English Electric had purchased for use as a test facility.

Meanwhile, the Air Ministry's enthusiasm for the aircraft had grown significantly, now that the prototype was nearing completion and its predicted performance capabilities were becoming clearer. By March 1949 the Air Ministry had settled on its initial requirements, stating: "It is not anticipated that there will be any inherent faults in the English Electric twin-jet which will not be

impossible of elimination in the production version, and that in order to ensure early delivery of the aircraft into service, a pilot order should now be placed. This would enable the firm to set up production lines and prepare the way for large-scale production when required. Five versions have been designed: Tactical bomber (B.5/47), Blind bomber (B.3/45), Target Marker bomber (B.22/48), Long range PR aircraft (PR.31/46) and Trainer (T.11/49). The most urgent need is for a jet bomber for Bomber Command for high speed and high altitude operations, and a PR aircraft to replace the Mosquito PR.34. Thus the initial requirement is for the B.22/48, PR.31/46 and the T.11/49. We are relying on this type for the re-armament of squadrons equipped with aircraft which are already outmoded; and if at all possible we wish to avoid placing orders for delivery in 1951 of

Beamont lifts VN799 into the air at Farnborough to begin what was one of the most astonishing spectacles that anyone had seen at the show. During the next few minutes he demonstrated that despite being a bomber, the A.1 possessed the handling qualities and performance of a jet fighter. It was a demonstration that sealed the aircraft's future and contributed towards America's later decision to buy it for USAF service.
(Photo: Aeroplane)

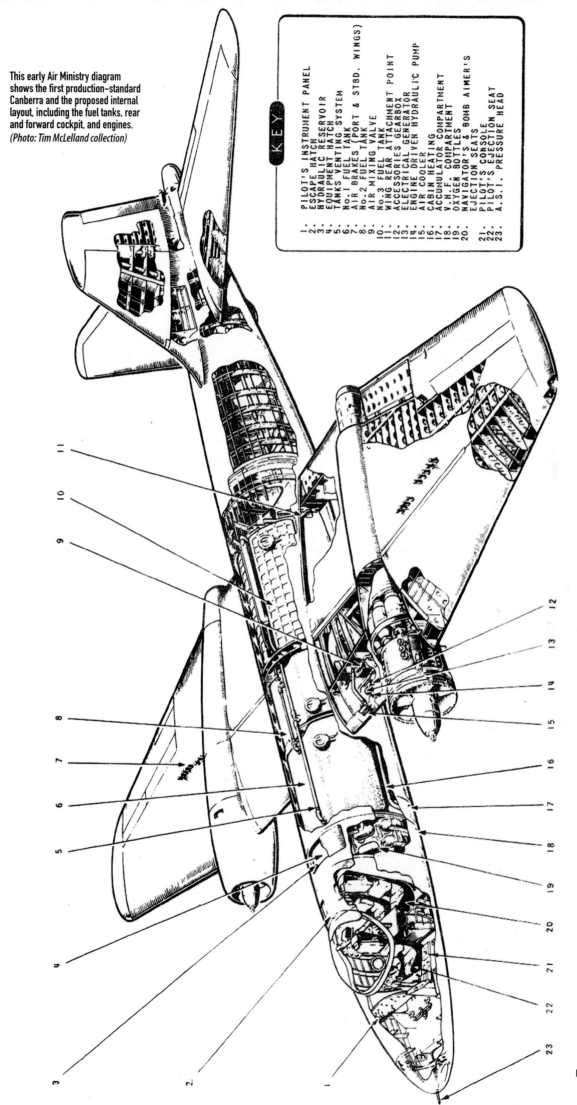

This early Air Ministry diagram shows the first production-standard Canberra and the proposed internal layout, including the fuel tanks, rear and forward cockpit, and engines.
(Photo: Tim McLelland collection)

KEY

1. PILOT'S INSTRUMENT PANEL
2. ESCAPE HATCH
3. HYDRAULIC RESERVOIR
4. EQUIPMENT HATCH
5. TANKS VENTING SYSTEM
6. No.1 FUEL TANK
7. AIR BRAKES (PORT & STBD. WINGS)
8. No.2 FUEL TANK
9. AIR MIXING VALVE
10. No.3 FUEL TANK
11. WING REAR ATTACHMENT POINT
12. ACCESSORIES GEARBOX
13. ELECTRICAL GENERATOR
14. ENGINE DRIVEN HYDRAULIC PUMP
15. AIR COOLER
16. CABIN HEATING
17. ACCUMULATOR COMPARTMENT
18. V.H.F. COMPARTMENT
19. OXYGEN BOTTLES
20. NAVIGATOR'S & BOMB AIMER'S EJECTION SEATS
21. PILOT'S CONSOLE
22. PILOT'S EJECTION SEAT
23. A.S.I. PRESSURE HEAD

By the time of the SBAC show at Farnborough in September 1949, it had already been agreed that the A.1 was to be named 'Canberra' and a suitable inscription was applied on the aircraft's nose. However, the aircraft wasn't officially named until many weeks later. *(Photo: Tim McLelland collection)*

Test pilot Roland Beamont inside the cockpit of VN799 shortly after the aircraft's first flight. The original, unmodified canopy is still fitted, missing the metal shroud that was subsequently fitted to cure minor turbulence problems. *(Photo: Tim McLelland collection)*

obsolete aircraft to maintain our squadrons until new production can give satisfactory numbers of jet types." It was proposed that the initial order comprised 30 B.22/48s, 30 PR.31/46s, and 15 T.11/49s.

On 1 March 1949 a contract was placed for 132 aircraft, which was quite an achievement for English Electric, when the prototype had still not even flown. In fact, the order illustrated not only supreme confidence in the design, but also the growing sense of urgency for Bomber Command and the British government. The RAF had barely begun to relinquish its wartime Lancaster bombers and was now equipped with only the Avro Lincoln as a direct replacement. The Lincoln was, of course, little more than an improved

Lancaster, and as the Cold War began to unfold it became abundantly clear that this obsolescent aircraft would be no credible deterrent against perceived Soviet intentions. The new jet bomber was needed and it was needed fast.

It was at this critical stage that the Air Ministry finally accepted that its plans to equip the A.1 with radar bombing equipment were simply not going to be achieved. Development of a suitable system (the H2S Mk.9) was dogged with delays and difficulties and a prevailing sense of urgency finally persuaded the RAF to revert to more traditional solutions, outlined in 1947's Specification B5/47. The A.1 bomber's projected radar-equipped nose compartment was abandoned and the

planned arrangement for a two-man crew was changed to incorporate a third crew member who would be responsible for visual bomb aiming by means of a clear nose section using a system based on the tried-and-tested T2 bombsight. The new third crew member would have to crawl into the A.1's small nose section and lay in a prone position to peer out of a clear Perspex window in much the same way as the RAF's wartime crew members had done, although he would be afforded the relative luxury of his own ejection seat, fixed beside the navigator's seat, behind the pilot. It wasn't an ideal arrangement but it was the best solution available. It had no effect on the aircraft's projected performance but it maintained a rather uncomfortable

VN799 with everything down, as Beamont makes a slow pass over the runway at Farnborough. The aircraft's slow-speed performance was facilitated by the deployment of landing flaps, two of which were installed in each wing, under the centre and inboard trailing edges. *(Photo: Aeroplane)*

Photographed during the middle of what was arguably the most important moment in the Canberra's history, VN799 races skywards in the hands of test pilot Roland Beamont, during its spectacular first demonstration at the 1949 SBAC Farnborough show. *(Photo: Aeroplane)*

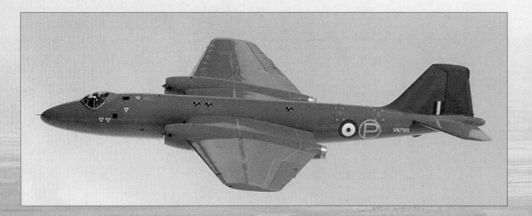

The celebrate the Canberra's 50th anniversary in 1999, No.39(1 PRU) Squadron repainted the last operational T.Mk.4 trainer (WJ874) to represent the Canberra prototype VN799 (left and main image). Although the Mk.4 exhibits some minor differences from the prototype, the aircraft is externally almost identical to VN799 and with a suitably authentic paint scheme the prototype's clean lines were successfully replicated. The livery was retained beyond retirement and into preservation.
(Photos: Crown copyright/RAF)

connection with old-fashioned and outdated techniques that the RAF had hoped to relinquish.

On 29 April 1949 the first A.1 prototype emerged from the flight test shed (Hangar 25) at Warton to make its inaugural engine runs, equipped with RA.2 powerplants that had been delivered by Rolls-Royce during the previous month. These tests proceeded smoothly and on 8 May, Roland Beaumont, English Electric's chief test pilot took the aircraft out onto the airfield to begin a series of taxi trials. By the following day he was able to confidently allow the aircraft to make three gentle hops into the air during some fast runs of up to 80kts, one lasting for some 500 yards. However, it was on the auspicious day of Friday, 13 May that weather conditions were deemed suitable and Beamont finally took VN799 into the air for its first true flight, accompanied by a Vampire chase plane. Much to observers' delight the flight went well and after returning from this short shake-down (which took the aircraft up to 10,000 feet) Beamont reported no major difficulties; indeed, his only major concern was the performance of the aircraft's rudder controls which suggested that the rudder hinge might be over-balanced, creating large yawing movements for relatively small rudder pedal inputs. This minor problem was resolved by reducing the height of the (wooden) rudder horn balance over a series

Canberra T.Mk.4 WJ877 had been repainted to represent VN799 for the Canberra's 40th anniversary in 1989. However, the scheme was applied with removable matt finish paint, in a vivid shade of blue that was rather different to that applied to VN799. The accuracy of this replication of VN799's colours and those of the other aircraft shown on this spread is a subject of some debate even now. There are still those who feel the 1989 effort is more accurate a shade than 1999's. Sadly, the aircraft was destroyed on 18 March 1991 when it crashed following loss of control during a simulated engine failure after take-off. All three crew were killed.
(Photo: Michael Freer)

of flights until the original curved fin top slowly changed into the familiar flattened shape employed on all subsequent aircraft. Beamont also reported that the cockpit had been uncomfortably warm, thanks to the huge one-piece 'bubble' canopy that acted rather like a small greenhouse. It was a seemingly minor complaint, but the aircraft's unusual cockpit canopy and its associated demisting issues, distorted vision difficulties and heating effects proved to be problems that frustrated aircrew throughout the

aircraft's operational life. The A.1's second test flight revealed the presence of elevator flutter (self-induced movement which increases in amplitude unless checked) and some time was spent modifying the tailplane surfaces and elevator balances until both the rudder and tailplanes functioned perfectly. A "collar" fairing was introduced behind the pilot's canopy to reduce local turbulence, curing a slight snaking (yaw) tendency that had also manifested itself on some test flights. But in

most respects the aircraft performed brilliantly and quickly demonstrated the 40,000ft altitude performance that had been laid-down by the Air Ministry. Likewise, the required 450kts top speed was exceeded by more than 20kts, and it was clear that later production aircraft with more powerful engines would be able to offer even greater performance. For the RAF, with a moribund fleet of aged Mosquitos, Lancasters and Lincolns, the jet prototype's performance seemed almost eye-watering. ❖

TESTING TIMES

English Electric's A.1 project continues to grow, while the RAF eagerly awaits the arrival of the new jet bomber

The second Canberra prototype VN813 racing skywards during the 1957 SBAC show at Farnborough. Fitted with a Spectre rocket motor, the aircraft was used as a test bed by de Havilland until 1959, when the aircraft was withdrawn. *(Photo: Aeroplane)*

Binbrook in 1951, shortly after the arrival of the first Canberras into RAF service. Early production B.Mk.2 aircraft WD930 and WD931 are pictured on a snowy field accompanied by the third Canberra prototype, VN828, together with a Lincoln from No.101 Squadron. (Photo: Tim McLelland collection)

Canberra B.Mk.2 WD962 was originally destined for the RAF but was delivered to the Royal Aircraft Establishment for ejection seat trials during January 1952. It remained with the RAE until 1961, when it was scrapped. (Photo: Tim McLelland collection)

Although the Canberra became famous as a twin-jet design, the A.1 was initially drawn up around a single, relatively powerful and physically huge centrifugal-flow engine, a concept Rolls-Royce persuaded English Electric to abandon. However, the early A.1 concept lasted only briefly, as a new company brochure was issued, showing the aircraft with two engines buried in the wing roots. According to the brochure, it was the rapid development of jet power units that had led the English Electric team to re-examine its design and convert it

into 'an improved proposal of the same general size and type'. The new engines were two axial Rolls-Royce AJ.65s that were basic, undeveloped versions of what became the classic Avon. These were of considerably smaller frontal area than the monstrous centrifugal engine meaning they could be almost completely buried in the wing root. Although the wing profile had to be increased to 15 per cent at the root but the intakes were so designed that the effective thickness of the wing never exceeded 12 per cent. At this stage the main undercarriage

units were also moved closer to the aircraft centreline, taking advantage of the extra wing depth that had been created.

Although this development process resulted in an aircraft visibly different to the design that had first been proposed, the simple contours of the original A.1 were retained, reflecting Petter's preference for simplicity. Even with two engines, the basic tubular fuselage was unchanged, as was the cockpit and tail layout, and even with two engines, the wing design was only modified where necessary. The advantages of two ➤

Canberra production in full flow, with six B.Mk.2 aircraft nearing completion, two PR.Mk.3 to the right of the photo, and tail sections from a further four Canberras visible in the background. The lead aircraft is finished in an early Bomber Command two-tone grey camouflage scheme, while the PR.Mk.3 is being completed in a PRU blue and grey finish. Both camouflage schemes were relatively short-lived. *(Photo: Aeroplane)*

The sole Canberra B.Mk.5 was the prototipe VX185. Manufactured as a PR.Mk.3 it was completed as a Canberra Mk.5 before making its first flight on 6 July 1951. When the proposed B.Mk.5 version was cancelled, VX185 was converted to Mk.8 standard and used as a trials aircraft by Ferranti, Shorts and Boulton Paul. *(Photo: Tim McLelland collection)*

engines were obvious, although the company brochure stated that even though the revised design had twin-engine reliability, the company did not altogether concede that such a precaution was necessary with jet engines.

However, the employment of two engines mounted within wing nacelles also provided greater flexibility for the installation of later types of engine, and this was an advantage which paid handsome dividends, as numerous aircraft were eventually used as flying test beds, fitted with almost every example of new British jet engine designs as they gradually emerged.

Removal of the engine from the fuselage allowed Petter's team to give the aircraft a bomb bay of substantially increased overall dimensions that could carry many combinations of bombs, up to and including a single 8,000lb weapon. The more efficient

axial engines enjoyed lower specific fuel consumption, and so the aircraft's fuel tankage was slightly reduced and the cells above the bomb bay were therefore simplified in design. The elimination of the long fuselage jet pipe enabled a simpler and lighter tailplane to be installed, and this also saved a considerable amount of weight in the aircraft's aft section. This weight saving required a reduction in the length of the front fuselage, but this was done without any reduction in the available stowage space as the former engine bay had now become available for both bomb loads and fuel.

Data on high-subsonic aerodynamics was now available (having been gathered in Germany by the Allies at the end of the war), and an alternative layout to the basic design was explored, incorporating a 30° swept-wing. This would have raised the aircraft's critical speed by about 35mph at 40,000ft

and with a more forward position now occupied by the engines and heavy wing roots, an even more compact fuselage became possible. But there were also disadvantages to this proposal and although Petter and his team regarded the German research as exciting, there was a great concern that too many aspects of swept wing design were still unknown, and this could have delayed the aircraft's development quite considerably. For example, wingtip stalling was causing trouble on new swept tailless designs (the DH.108 and AW.52) and sweepback invariably increases the wing's structural weight. In any case, the aircraft's envisaged maximum speed suggested that it would not be affected by compressibility, owing to the relatively modest total thrust provided by the two engines. Consequently, interest in developing the A.1 beyond its most basic

Second prototype Canberra VN813 is pictured at the 1957 Farnborough show, performing a low pass with its Spectre rocket motor ignited. After being operated by Rolls Royce at Hucknall for Nene engine development, VN813 was modified to carry the Spectre motor at Chilbolton and operated from Hatfield until its withdrawal in 1959. *(Photo: David Webster www.the-best-of-british.com)*

Canberra B.Mk.2 WH671 was assigned to Boulton Paul for engine de-icing trials before being transferred to Rolls-Royce, where it was used during development of the RA.14 Avon engine. It remained in service until 1961, when it was scrapped. *(Photo: Tim McLelland collection)*

proportions was not pursued and in retrospect was probably a wise decision, not least because it endowed the aircraft with a versatility far beyond anything that was envisaged at the time of its creation.

When compared with the single-engine design, the gross weight of the twin-engine was reduced by more than ten percent, to less than 40,000lb. This was largely due to the reduction in power plant weight (even with two being fitted), lower fuel consumption and the improvement in fuselage design and the consequent structural savings. The wing area was reduced from 1,040 to 950 square feet, without increasing the wing loading, and the aspect ratio was correspondingly reduced from 5.4 to 4.9. There were also some detail design changes in the pressure cabin. The navigator was now placed behind the pilot, facing forward and connected with his colleague by a narrow gangway on the

starboard side. This small amount of space became particularly useful when the decision to abandon a blind bombing capability was made, as it enabled a bomb aimer to gain direct access to the nose compartment, where a clear Perspex nose cone was fitted to provide a visual bombing capability. Unusually, an optically flat clear panel was designed for incorporation within the nose cone but it was positioned offset to starboard, so that sufficient internal space would be available for the bomb aimer and his visual bombing equipment. The proposed radar scanner was to have been housed entirely within the lower half of the nose and so the twin-wheel nose gear had been moved back and arranged to retract vertically behind the Pressure bulkhead, and this arrangement was not changed. A new design brochure was submitted late in 1945 to the Ministry of Supply to meet the B.3/45

specification, and on January 7 1946, the contract for four (prototype) English Electric A.1 aircraft had been placed. It was at this time that Petter and his strengthened design and development team moved to Warton, finally abandoning their rather basic offices that had been set-up above a bus garage in Preston's Corporation Street. However, conditions at Warton were hardly any better, even though the United States Army Air Force had at least made the site habitable before their departure, having even installed a very effective central heating system that proved to be rather too excessive for British tastes. Design and development work got underway at Warton in great secrecy, but long before the first flight of the A.1, it became an open secret (at least in the British aircraft industry) that the English Electric Company were designing a new aeroplane, and that it was to be a very significant one.

Production of the Canberra was concentrated at English Electric's Samlesbury works, but in order to meet Bomber Command's urgent need for the aircraft (and a gradual requirement to manufacture aircraft for export), additional production was sub-contracted to Avro, Handley Page and Shorts. As can be seen in these photos taken inside the Shorts factory at Sydenham, there was a rather bizarre contrast between the sleek and modern Canberra jet bomber, and the elderly Sunderland flying boats that were still being refurbished there. *(Photos: Aeroplane)*

Initial training on the Canberra was conducted by the Jet Conversion Unit, based at Binbrook, as illustrated by this photograph taken in January 1952. In addition to Canberras (WD951 is seen here) the unit operated a small fleet of single and twin-seat Meteors. *(Photo: Tim McLelland collection)*

Completed in June 1951, Canberra B.Mk.2 WD938 was delivered to No.101 Squadron at Binbrook. It was subsequently assigned to No.231 OCU before joining the Near East Air Force (NEAF) in Cyprus, where it remained in use until 1970. *(Photo: Tim McLelland collection)*

Fifth production Canberra PR.Mk.3 WE139 was one of five aircraft assigned to a London-to-New Zealand air race staged in October 1953. As the outright winner, WE139 was suitably adorned with a record of its achievement, painted on its nose. It went on to serve with No.39 squadron in Aden, and is now on permanent display at the Royal Air Force Museum, Hendon. *(Photo: Tim McLelland collection).*

Furthest from the camera in this line-up of Canberras is B.Mk.2 WH715, an aircraft that was operated on test duties at Boscombe Down, Defford, Seighford, West Freugh and Farnborough, before crashing in October 1968. The penultimate aircraft is PR.Mk.3 WE135, an aircraft operated by No.231 OCU and also used on a variety of test programmes. In the middle is T.Mk.4 WH846, operated by No.231 OCU and No.100 Squadron. It is now on display at the Yorkshire Air Museum. Canberra B.Mk.6 WJ755 was engaged in test flying until it was withdrawn in 1961, while B.Mk.6 WH797 was eventually withdrawn from RAF service and converted to T.Mk.22 standard for the Royal Navy. *(Photo: Aeroplane)*

Other developmental proposals were considered from a very early stage, and the concept of creating a civil aircraft was looked at in some detail. A study made in October 1946 described a 34-passenger airliner for short haul flights of between 490 and 930 miles, depending on the operating altitude employed, with a maximum range of some 1,600 miles with 16 passengers. This interesting design was a straightforward development of the A.1 project with the same wing design and an enlarged fuselage giving an interior diameter of 10ft. The cabin was pressurized and soundproofed and entirely unbroken by structural components. The seats were arranged in orthodox style in pairs on either side of the gangway. Baggage was to be stored under the floor within the pressure hull (for structural convenience) in a space estimated at 320 cubic feet. In order to take full advantage of this freight hold, it was proposed to load baggage and cargo on to a series of trays that would then to be pushed along the length of the freight compartment on tracks. This allowed the size of the

compartment door to be kept to a minimum, and it was suggested that baggage should be pre-loaded on to special trays immediately on arrival at the airport, so that embarkation time could be kept as short as possible. It was to have been powered by two Rolls-Royce AJ.65s, each of 6,500lb thrust, boosted by a further 1,000lb for take off. Later development was envisaged by installing more powerful engines. The original AJ.65s would have given the aircraft a cruising speed of about 450 mph, which would have put the aircraft in the same performance category as the early Comet airliners, although the English Electric aircraft would have had a much shorter range.

A huge amount of specialized equipment was needed for ground-testing the new A.1, including mechanical test facilities of all kinds, computers (which were still in their infancy) and of course, wind tunnels. This equipment was vitally important, and thankfully the board of directors of English Electric immediately accepted this, and substantial sums of money were allocated for

it. It marked the beginning of the company's investment in equipment and technology which continued over subsequent years and enabled the company to gradually develop into what is now the United Kingdom's home of military aircraft design, more than half a century later (as part of BAE Systems). But it was not just the equipment that enabled them to produce what was a very advanced flying machine for its time. The other essential ingredient of the design team was the ability to interpret and apply the information that this new equipment provided. It was at once foreseen that a tremendous range of test equipment would be needed to carry through the long bomber development programme. Three tunnels were built; a 9ft x 7ft low-speed unit, a jet-induced high-speed tunnel and a water tunnel. The low-speed tunnel became operative in May 1948, the high-speed tunnel some two months later and the water tunnel in March 1949. These played a major part in the A.1 programme, but they were only part of a wide range of facilities that were

available to the design team. There was a large structural test frame in which a complete A.1 wing was installed, and which later tested a complete P.IA (Lightning) airframe to destruction. There was also a hydraulic rig to prove the endurance of the aircraft's hydraulics, and a whole range of other equipment. Nearly all the design and construction of these facilities was done by the English Electric Aircraft Division, with the help of other departments of the company. The jet tunnel was capable a dealing with all the speeds called for by the A.1, but it was later superseded by a supersonic tunnel, , for initial P.1 (Lightning) testing.

As described, the A.1 prototype made its maiden flight on May 13, 1949. Already ordered "off the drawing board" many months previously the aircraft was already in the early stages of quantity production when this maiden flight, place and, consequently, it was only 18 months later that the aircraft was in squadron service with No.101 Squadron of RAF Bomber Command at Binbrook in Lincolnshire. At the Society of British ➤

32

Most Canberra T.Mk.4 trainers were initially delivered to No.231 Operational Conversion Unit at Bassingbourn, formed in December 1951. Bomber Command's requirement for a large number of qualified Canberra crews kept the unit extremely busy, and numerous training accidents occurred, some due to a technical problem caused by a fault in the aircraft's tailplane trim actuating system, while many other mishaps were a result of novice pilots being unaccustomed to the aircraft's acceleration rate. However, the OCU's training system soon established a safe and successful regime and by the summer of 1956 the unit had organised its own formation display team. During the Coventry Air Pageant staged in July of that year, the unit's four Canberras performed a remarkable vertical bomb burst split at the end of their routine. *(Photos: Tim McLelland collection)*

Aircraft Constructors banquet in September 1949, Lord Tedder referred to the Canberra as a "good looking youngster" which would "soon be taking the place of the Lancasters, Stirlings, Halifaxes and Lincolns." He reminded his audience that, even at the end of the war, Germany was producing more fighters than Britain and the USA together, and therefore the ability of Britain to produce a modem bomber was hugely important. It was, he said, the "punch that was forecast" by the aircraft that "one's mind was at that time concentrated." But even before the first aircraft flew, the process of developing it still further had begun. The prototypes were only representative of the proposed production machines, although in most respects they were remarkably similar to the aircraft that followed, and only minor changes were made to the production-standard aircraft, after more significant alterations had already been made (primarily to the rudder, tailplane and canopy area) following the first flights. Even the sole Nene-powered prototype (VN813) eventually became redundant when progress with the Avon's development satisfied English Electric (and the Air Ministry) that an alternative wouldn't be needed. The only unusual aspect of the initial production process was the abandonment of the first operational variant that had been expected to enter RAF service. By the summer of 1949

the A.1 had unofficially been named "Canberra" and the first production aircraft would therefore be the Canberra B.Mk.1. But after the abandonment of the proposed blind bombing capability that the RAF had wanted and expected, the revised crew compartment and re-designed nose profile prompted English Electric to designate the re-designed aircraft as the Canberra B.Mk.2 and so, rather unusually, the RAF never acquired the first production variant of its own aircraft. Precisely when the A.1 was named "Canberra" is unclear but it is known that the name was chosen by English Electric's Chairman Sir George Nelson who subsequently explained that he was asked by the Air Ministry to suggest a name; "Being a fervent believer that the peace and happiness of the world depends on the unity and understanding of the British Commonwealth, I sat down to think of a suitable name for this machine to further that object, and chose Canberra, the capital of its farthest flung country, the Commonwealth of Australia. This was immediately accepted by the Air Council".

The afore-mentioned Farnborough show was the first occasion on which the public was able to see Britain's first jet bomber. Test pilot Roland Beamont devised a six-minute display routine for prototype VN799, based on his (and English Electric's) desire to demonstrate the potential of the new

aircraft. Until this stage it was believed (both by industry and military chiefs) that jet power would represent only a means of improving aircraft performance in relatively modest terms, either by increasing attainable altitudes or speeds. This belief was obviously based on many years of experience, and the slow, laborious way in which piston-engine aircraft had gradually been improved through the wartime years. The advent of the jet engine had demonstrated that both fighter and bomber aircraft would continue to develop still further, but few people imagined that there would ever be any quantum leaps in capability. But English Electric's team already knew that the Canberra was different. Despite being a bomber, the aircraft was relatively small and with a clean aerodynamic design, a very large wing area and two relatively powerful engines, it was capable of achieving a performance that was superior to many of its fighter aircraft contemporaries. Farnborough was Beamont's opportunity to demonstrate this to the world. His efforts were initially thwarted by a simple mistake, and as the aircraft prepared to take-off on its very first display, the engines suddenly wound-down to a standstill. Beamont had taxied to the runway with an almost-empty fuel tank selected, and had failed to switch to other

RAF Scampton, June 1954, with No.27 Squadron's Canberra B.Mk.2 bombers on display to media photographers, starting engines to illustrate the Canberra's distinctive cartridge system smoke. As can be seen, Scampton's concrete runway had yet to be laid, and without the numerous hard standings that were constructed for Vulcans a decade later, the unit's Canberras are parked on grass. At the time that these photographs were taken, these Canberras were being used as support aircraft and photographic platforms for filming of the famous Dambusters movie. *(Photos: Aeroplane)*

The first Canberra B.Mk.2 VX165 made its first flight on 21 April 1950. It enjoyed only a brief time in the air and crashed on 15 August 1951 at Boscombe Down. Following a stall warning on approach to the airfield, the pilot applied engine power but the starboard engine responded more rapidly than the port engine and an uncontrollable roll ensured, causing the port wing to strike the runway. It was returned to English Electric by road and stripped of spares before being scrapped. *(Photo: Aeroplane)*

Colour images of the earliest of the RAF's Canberra B.Mk.2 aircraft are rare. This RAF publicity photograph shows a trio of aircraft, those at the front and rear operated by No.61 Squadron, a unit that re-equipped with Canberras in 1952. The middle aircraft is from No. 109 Squadron.

WH718 was one of many RAF Canberras involved in Operation Musketeer during 1956 whilst serving with No.15 Squadron. Like many other Canberras, the aircraft was repainted with yellow and black identification markings whilst flying bombing missions over Egypt from bases in Malta and Cyprus. Many years later it was converted into a TT.Mk.18 target tug and remained in RAF service until 1990. *(Photo: Tim McLelland collection)*

Canberra T.Mk.4 prototype WN467, pictured en route to the 1952 SBAC Farnborough show where it was displayed in typically flamboyant style by test pilot Roland Beamont. The aircraft entered RAF service with No.231 OCU and went on to join Station Flights at Binbrook, Honington, Wittering and Bruggen, where it was retired in 1971. *(Photo: Tim McLelland collection)*

full fuel tanks before fuel supply ran out. It was an embarrassing debut that frustrated Beamont and angered Petter, but the SBAC show organisers agreed to allow Beamont to fly at the end of that day's flying display, and late in the afternoon of 6 September the prototype Canberra VN799 literally leapt into the air. With a take-off run of only 600 yards, Beamont held the aircraft low over the runway before pulling sharply skywards into a climbing turn, heading back towards the airfield at a seemingly alarming speed. He immediately lowered the aircraft until it was just 100 ft above the runway and raced past the astonished spectators before pulling into a vertical climb. Rolling off the top of the climb, the Canberra roared back towards the crowd, where Beamont performed a neat 360-degree roll at less than 300 ft above the runway. Returning at a lower speed with the aircraft's landing gear extended and bomb doors open, Beamont rolled the aircraft sharply from side to side before applying power and entering another steep climb into a half loop, after which the landing gear came down once more and the Canberra turned steeply over Farnborough's famous black sheds, before touching down. It was an incredible spectacle. Bomber aircraft were

large, cumbersome machines that lumbered into the air and had to be coaxed through gentle turns and hauled into long, tedious climbs. The Canberra had raced around the show site like no other aircraft that had preceded it. It was faster and more manoeuvrable than a fighter, and yet this was to be the RAF's new bomber. The media loved it. The public was spellbound, while the SBAC display committee didn't know what to think. Inevitably, concerns were expressed that Beamont had been taking unnecessary risks in display the Canberra so

flamboyantly, and Vickers test pilot "Mutt" Summers was asked to "have a word" with Beamont. However, Summers knew only too well that Beamont had performed his display routine with skill and precision, and it was the Canberra's capabilities that had enabled him to make such an impression. No changes were made to the display routine and for the rest of the show week the assembled spectators were again treated to a daily demonstration of just what an amazing machine English Electric had produced. ❖

Canberra PR.Mk.3 WE146 pictured over Hampshire during the 1953 SBAC Farnborough show. This particular aircraft didn't enter regular RAF service and was used by the RAE for camera trials. It then joined the Meteorological Research Flight and finally went to Llanbedr where it was withdrawn in 1973. *(Photo: Aeroplane)*

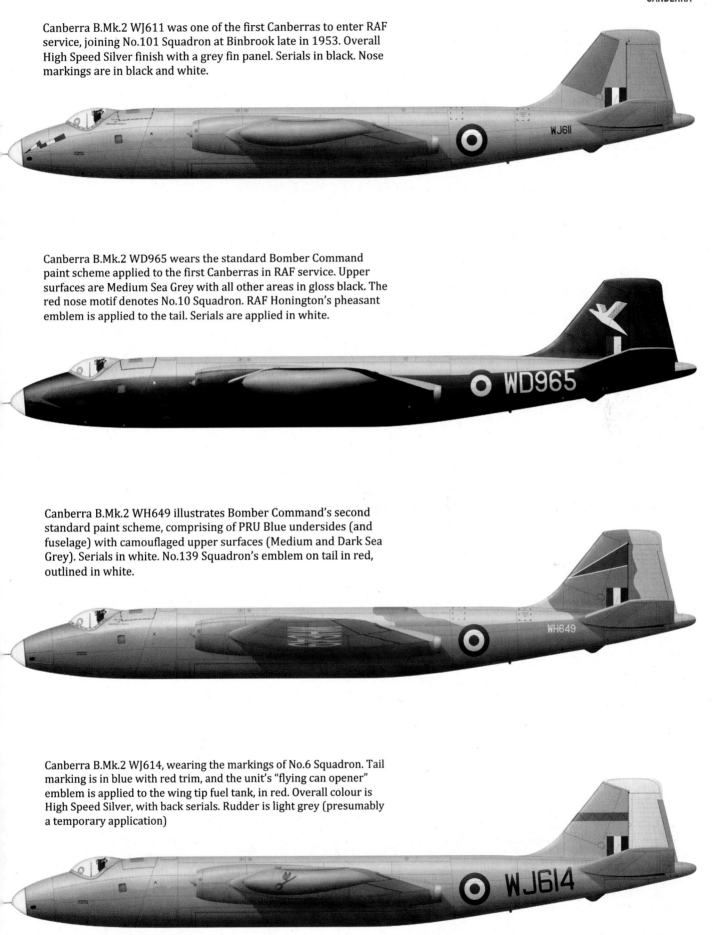

Canberra B.Mk.2 WJ611 was one of the first Canberras to enter RAF service, joining No.101 Squadron at Binbrook late in 1953. Overall High Speed Silver finish with a grey fin panel. Serials in black. Nose markings are in black and white.

Canberra B.Mk.2 WD965 wears the standard Bomber Command paint scheme applied to the first Canberras in RAF service. Upper surfaces are Medium Sea Grey with all other areas in gloss black. The red nose motif denotes No.10 Squadron. RAF Honington's pheasant emblem is applied to the tail. Serials are applied in white.

Canberra B.Mk.2 WH649 illustrates Bomber Command's second standard paint scheme, comprising of PRU Blue undersides (and fuselage) with camouflaged upper surfaces (Medium and Dark Sea Grey). Serials in white. No.139 Squadron's emblem on tail in red, outlined in white.

Canberra B.Mk.2 WJ614, wearing the markings of No.6 Squadron. Tail marking is in blue with red trim, and the unit's "flying can opener" emblem is applied to the wing tip fuel tank, in red. Overall colour is High Speed Silver, with back serials. Rudder is light grey (presumably a temporary application)

Drawings by Chris Sandham-Bailey (www.inkworm.co.uk)

INTO SERVICE

The Canberra joins the ranks of the Royal Air Force

WD930 (the second production B.Mk.2) was operated by the RAF Handling Squadron at Manby before joining Rolls-Royce at Hucknall where it was fitted with Avon RA.7s, RA.14s, RA.16s and finally RA.29s, the latter engine being destined for the Comet airliner. As part of this test work the engines were fitted with a series of silencer designs. *(Photo: Aeroplane)*

Trials employing the prototype VN799 continued into the winter of 1949, by which stage the Nene-powered second prototype had also been completed. The third followed shortly afterwards on 22 November, flying not from Warton but from English Electric's long-established factory airfield at Samlesbury where it had been built, a few miles to the north. The fourth machine introduced a revised fuel system including the addition of wingtip-mounted external fuel tanks that allowed for an additional 500 gallons of fuel at the expense of very little drag; the tanks could be jettisoned in flight if necessary. So successful were these tanks that they became a common sight. The first of these aircraft was VX165 and it took to the air on 21 April 1950. With tip tanks fitted, the bomb aimer's clear

◄ Armstrong Siddeley Motors flew Canberra WD933 as a test bed for its Sapphire engine. Three types of Sapphire were installed, culminating in the 10,300lb thrust ASSa.7, in August 1954. Three months later, the aircraft suffered a spectacular crash at Bitteswell. It flipped onto its back during an emergency belly landing and slid inverted across the airfield. The pilot and observer escaped unhurt. *(Photo: Tim McLelland collection)*

nose section incorporated and third crew seat installed, this aircraft dispensed with the small dorsal fin that had been present on the previous prototypes, after test results confirmed that it was unnecessary.

A crash on 13 June 1951 cut VX165's contribution to the flight test programme short. Resulting from an engine fire, the accident was not attributable to any design flaw and the test programme continued without delay, so that by 1951 English Electric's A.1 was ready for its customer – the Royal Air Force. As explained previously, it was the company's Chairman Sir George Nelson who decided upon 'Canberra' as a suitable name for the bomber. Keen to foster relations between Britain and the Commonwealth (and with the clear possibility of export orders in mind too) the bomber was officially named after Australia's capital city on 19 January 1951 at a ceremony attended by the Australian Prime Minister at Biggin Hill, where the first production Canberra (WD929) was placed on show.

It was sad to note that this celebratory naming event did not include the presence of Petter, as he had resigned from English Electric ten months previously and no longer

had any association with the company. Despite being a very talented designer, Petter did not settle into English Electric's management structure with any confidence and his time at Warton was often dogged with disagreements between him and the engineering team at Strand Road. Eventually he had asked for the two facilities to be separated and his 'go it alone' philosophy did not sit well with English Electric's management. The continual disagreements inevitably meant that he would resign, but his departure was a less-than-happy one, and he actively encouraged members of his team to go with him to his new post at Folland Aircraft. Some of the team accepted his offer and it was Freddie Page who subsequently assumed control of the Canberra's design and development – and of course the creation of the 'Lighting' interceptor that followed it.

But despite the regrettable events at Warton, the Canberra's production continued and on 25 May 1951, Beamont took Canberra B.Mk.2 WD936 to Binbrook in Lincolnshire, where he executed another brilliant display that amazed and delighted the onlookers, most of whom were associated with the many Lincoln bombers that were ➤

Canberra B.Mk.2 WD952 was assigned to Bristol Engines at Filton in December 1951. Its Avon engines were replaced with 8,000lb thrust Olympus 99s, derated from 9,750lb to suit the Canberra's airframe limitations. In May 1953 the aircraft established a world record, reaching an altitude of 63,668ft. It climbed to 65,876ft three months later under the power of 12,000lb thrust Olympus 102s designed for the Vulcan. WD952 crashed in March 1956 and was taken to Colerne for scrapping.
(Photos: FAST Museum & Aeroplane)

➤ Following the loss of WD952, Bristol acquired Canberra B.Mk.2 WH713 in January 1957. Formerly with No.15 Squadron, the aircraft was modified with extended engine nacelles accommodating Olympus 104 engines rated at 13,000lb thrust each. It was also employed for engine silencer testing before being withdrawn and scrapped at Filton in September 1959.
(Photos: Aeroplane)

scattered around the airfield. As they stood beside their obsolete monsters, they couldn't fail to be impressed by the sprightly Canberra, rolling and looping high in the skies above the Lincolnshire Wolds. Beamont duly landed and taxied in and handed the aircraft to No.101 Squadron. This was to become the RAF's first jet bomber squadron but the Canberra had already made its noisy presence apparent to everyone some weeks previously, when WD951 had arrived to join the newly formed Jet Conversion Flight, created to introduce Lincoln pilots to the challenges of jet-powered flight. A standard Canberra B.Mk.2, WD951 was of little use as a conversion trainer, so a pair of dual-control Meteor T.Mk.7 jets joined the flight, allowing crews to become familiar with the peculiarities of jet power before flying the Canberra. It was quickly established that there were in fact very few challenges to be met and training for the fledgling Canberra pilots proved to be straightforward.

Through the first year of operations at Binbrook only one significant accident occurred when WD938 ran out of fuel and made a wheels-up landing on the airfield. The flight eventually became part of No.617

Squadron, the second of Binbrook's Canberra units, followed in due course by Nos 9, 50, and 101 Squadrons. When all of these units had completed transition onto the Canberra, Binbrook almost became an all-Canberra base. Despite the station's remote location out in the wilds of Lincolnshire (and the presence of some remaining Lincolns that lingered in service until the Vickers Valiant was introduced), Binbrook became a popular destination for countless RAF and other military and government officials, all of whom wanted to witness the world's first jet bomber base in operation. However by 1953 attention began to shift some miles south to Coningsby, where Nos 15, 44, 57, and 149 Squadrons had been operating Boeing Washington bombers (the adopted British name for the Superfortress) for a couple of years. In an effort to improve Bomber Command's capabilities, these Washingtons had been leased from the USA so that at least part of Bomber Command was able to operate an aircraft that had a more plausible chance of presenting a serious deterrent to the USSR. The Washington had the ability to successfully deliver weapons to the heart of the Soviet Union if necessary, whereas the

RAF's Lincoln had increasingly become almost an embarrassment, its outward wartime appearance only serving to confirm that the RAF was still operating an aircraft that was at least a decade out-of-date.

The Washington was in reality no more advanced than the Lincoln, but as a far bigger and more powerful machine it did at least have the ability to fly further and higher, and deliver a meaningful bomb load. The Canberra, however, represented a leap into a whole new era, and replacement of the Washingtons gave the Coningsby wing a completely new type of aeroplane that possessed breathtaking speed and agility, and an altitude capability that was (by contemporary standards) unbeatable. But it is also true that the Canberra was not a strategic bomber. Designed for a tactical role, it didn't have the fuel capacity necessary to fly deep into the heart of the USSR, and although Bomber Command proposed to use the aircraft as a conventional medium-level bomber, it would eventually be mostly employed in support of ground operations, and not as an entirely independent strike force. As a credible deterrent against the Soviet threat it was undoubtedly an aircraft ➤

Rolls-Royce conducted early engine reheat trials with Meteor RA435, and Canberra B.Mk.2 WD943 was assigned to Hucknall in October 1951 to continue the work. A pair of afterburning Avon RA.7R engines was initially installed and eventually replaced by more powerful RA.14R engines. The aircraft remained in use with Rolls-Royce until July 1957, when it was ferried to No.23 Maintenance Unit and scrapped.
(Photos: Aeroplane)

to be reckoned with, because it had the ability to fly high and fly fast, so even if it was not a direct threat to – for example – the heart of downtown Moscow, it was not to be dismissed. If a conflict broke out in Europe, the Canberra would have been a very serious threat to any Soviet advance, capable of reaching and destroying almost any target of significance within the European theatre. Just as significantly, the RAF regarded the Canberra not just as a declared capability in itself, but also a major step towards an even more advanced bomber force that would emerge just a few years later when the new V-Bombers - The Valiant, Vulcan, and Victor came into service. As the Coningsby Wing re-equipped with Canberras, it was probably unclear to many observers that the new jet bomber's stay would in fact be relatively brief, and that it would soon make way for an even bigger, noisier and deadlier machine.

Scampton was the third base to re-equip with Canberras (during 1953) and Marham duly followed so that by 1954 Bomber Command could boast a force of 16 operational Canberra squadrons. The RAF now had a credible force of very capable jet bombers at its disposal. This status also enabled the RAF to begin the task of training crews not only for the Canberra force itself, but so that an even greater number of aircrew would be ready to take on the new V-Force bombers that would be coming into service. Nobody doubted that the task of operating the new (and large) force of strategic bombers would be a major challenge, and the new Canberra squadrons were regarded as an ideal 'stepping stone' on the path towards creating a good supply of capable and qualified air and ground crews who were familiar and confident with all aspects of jet bomber operations.

Of course, the RAF therefore needed to train a huge number of crews to fly the Canberra and in order to meet this task No.231 Operational Conversion Unit was formed at Bassingbourn. The unit was initially equipped with a variety of aircraft types until the first Canberras were delivered, and full-scale training didn't get underway until the first Canberra T.Mk.4 dual-control aircraft were delivered, starting in August 1953. A contract issued in September 1950 covered the first batch of Canberra T.Mk.4 trainers, and the first production aircraft (WE188) made its maiden flight on 30 October 1952 and was duly delivered to Bassingbourn. The Canberra T.Mk.4 was outwardly very similar to the B2. The same fuselage structure and canopy were unaltered, but a solid nose was

substituted for the bomber's clear section. The student occupied the pilot's seat to port, with the instructor sitting directly to the right. The navigator's seat in the rear of the cockpit was retained and in order to enable both the student and navigator to reach their seats, the instructor's seat was designed to swivel. It wasn't the most elegant of arrangements and to describe the T4's cockpit as cramped would be an understatement, but it was a simple and inexpensive means of enabling students to convert onto the Canberra with relative ease.

However, the OCU's early experience with the Canberra wasn't entirely trouble free. Various Canberras had been lost in accidents because of a common tailplane trim fault that took some time to identify and cure. But at

Although the Canberra B.Mk.5 radar-guided target marker variant was abandoned (judged to be unnecessary), the sole Mk.5 made many contributions towards the type's development. Having been converted from a PR.Mk.3 airframe, it was fitted with more powerful Avon RA.7 engines rated at 7,500lb. It also had integral wing fuel tanks, for an additional 900 gallons of available fuel. English Electric was keen to establish how this additional fuel might extend the aircraft's range and several long sorties (of five hours or more) were conducted around the UK. Eventually it was decided that a double transatlantic crossing would demonstrate the aircraft's range and this was achieved on 26 August 1952, when Beamont flew the aircraft from Aldergrove to Gander in Newfoundland. After a brief refuelling stop he returned, completing the round trip in just over ten hours. VX185 went on to become the prototype Canberra B(I).Mk.8.
(Photo: Aeroplane)

◄ ▲ Armstrong Siddeley received Canberra B.Mk.2 WK141 from the RAF in January 1955. It was used as a test bed for the company's Sapphire ASSa.7 engine until 1958, when it was modified to carry a single Viper 8 engine. The latter was being developed for multiple applications, including the Jet Provost trainer. The Viper was housed in a pod under the aircraft's wing and a more powerful variant was subsequently installed. WK141 was transferred to Filton before being withdrawn in 1963, when it went to Prestwick for fire rescue training.
(Photos: Aeroplane)

Canberra B.Mk.2 WK163 enjoyed a particularly interesting history. Completed in January 1955, it was assigned to Armstrong Siddeley for Sapphire engine testing, but towards the end of that year was modified to accept an example of the Napier Double Scorpion rocket motor that was being developed for potential use in English Electric's P.1. As part of the rocket test programme the aircraft was routinely climbed to remarkable altitudes, including a record 70,310ft on 28 August 1957. It was then used to test Viper engines before going to the Royal Radar Establishment, where it was fitted with Mk.6 wings and the forward fuselage section from XH568. When radar trials work at Pershore ended, WK163 was transferred to RAE Bedford and then to DRA Farnborough, in 1994. It was withdrawn from use a few months later and sold to Classic Aviation Projects. This group already owned XH568 and took this opportunity to reunite WK163 with its original nose section. Registered as G–BVWC, the aircraft became a popular attraction on the air show circuit in 1997, repainted in its original silver finish. It was subsequently repainted in a grey/black paint scheme, intended to represent an early Bomber Command machine. During 2000 it joined the Air Atlantique — later Classic Air Force — fleet at Coventry but suffered an engine failure in 2006 and remained grounded pending the acquisition of a replacement Avon. Hopes to return it to flying condition in 2015 were dashed and with the dissolution of the Classic Air Force, ownership of the partially dismantled airframe passed to the Vulcan to the Sky Trust in 2020. Late in 2023 it remained at the latter's Robin Hood Airport base, its future, like that of the airport, undecided. *(Photos: Aeroplane)*

the OCU there were also losses that couldn't be attributed to this deficiency and after a great deal of investigation it was established that students were deliberately flying the Canberras into the ground because of a tendency to misread the aircraft's artificial horizon in bad weather or at night. Having become accustomed to the laborious take-off acceleration of piston-engine aircraft, the Canberra's sprightly performance, combined with a misinterpretation of the instruments, fooled students into believing that the aircraft was climbing at a higher angle than recommended, and the nose was duly pointed downwards with catastrophic results. It was a simple error that could be resolved through better instruction but for some time there was a recurrent worry that jet bomber training wouldn't be as straightforward as had been imagined. In fact, the OCU at Bassingbourn succeeded in producing a seemingly endless stream of very capable crews for 18 years, after which the unit moved to Cottesmore and then to Wyton. When the OCU finally disbanded in 1993 it had trained more than 8,000 Canberra crews in total.

The RAF's re-equipment with Canberras continued at a steady pace with not only the standard B.Mk.2 bomber variant settling into service, but also the T.Mk.4 trainer and, eventually, the PR.Mk.3, a derivative of the bomber designed for photographic reconnaissance. Outwardly similar to the B.Mk.2, the PR.Mk.3 featured a 14in 'plug' in the forward fuselage (behind the cockpit) to enable six cameras to be fitted. Some additional fuel was also housed in the fuselage and this gave the PR3 more than 540 gallons of extra capacity, increasing the range to 3,585 miles. By 1954 the B.Mk.2 had been superseded by the B.Mk.6, fitted with a pair of uprated Avon Mk.109 engines, each delivering 7,500lb of thrust. The B.Mk.6 also introduced a 450-gallon integral fuel tank inside each wing. These improvements (combined with the new Maxaret anti-skid braking systems for the landing gear that improved landing performance) gave the Canberra an increased overall speed of a nominal 10kt and also increased the aircraft's range to 3,400 miles. The Canberra Mk.6 was manufactured by English Electric (at its Samlesbury factory) and by Short Brothers, based in Belfast (the B.Mk.2 was also built under license by both Shorts and Handley Page). The task of churning out a large fleet of jet bombers was beyond the capacity of English Electric in isolation, and with the Lightning interceptor now taking up more and more resources, it was inevitable that some Canberra B.Mk.6 production would be subcontracted. Ironically, English Electric ➤

Illustrating the range of armament available to the Canberra, this B(I).Mk.6 is positioned at the head of the Samlesbury assembly line with an array of weaponry laid before it. Included are a 20mm Hispano cannon pack, 500lb, 540lb and 1,000lb HE bombs, 2.7in SNEB rocket projectiles, General Electric Minigun ammunition, Matra rocket launchers, and 20/25lb practice bombs and their carriers. The Canberra could also carry several other weapons, including tactical atomic bombs. *(Photo: Tim McLelland collection)*

The Canberra B(I).Mk.6 was an interim design pending the delivery of the later Mk.8 interdictor variant. Based on the standard Canberra Mk.6 airframe, the B(I).Mk.6 was configured for low-level intruder operations with underwing weapons pylons and a ventral gun pack in the bomb bay. WT307 was manufactured at Samlesbury and spent two years on trials and evaluation flying before joining No.213 Squadron at Brüggen. It was returned to BAC in 1969 for possible refurbishment and resale but it remained in storage until it was scrapped in 1976. *(Photo: Aeroplane)*

Canberra PR.Mk.7 provides an interesting comparison with the previous photo of the Mk.6. The 14in fuselage extension incorporated into the PR.Mk.7 can be seen ahead of the WH799's wing leading edge, but in all other respects the aircraft is outwardly identical. A Syrian Meteor shot WH799 down on November 6, 1956 during the Suez Crisis. *(Photo: Aeroplane)*

XH570 was one of a batch of four Canberra B.Mk.6 aircraft manufactured in 1955. Modified to B.Mk.6(BS) standard, it was subsequently designated as a Mk.16, fitted with Blue Shadow sideways-looking radar. It is seen at Luqa, Malta wearing the flamboyant markings of No.6 Squadron. *(Photo: Godfrey Mangion)*

Canberra B.Mk.16 WT369 illustrates No.6 Squadron's markings as carried during the late 1960s and early 70s when the unit's aircraft were camouflaged for low-level operations. In addition to what appears to be a a rocket pack minus its nosecone under the wing. This aircraft was written off in a landing accident at Luqa during August 1968. *(Photo: Tim McLelland collection)*

A magnificent line-up of Canberra B.Mk.15s from No.45 Squadron, pictured on the flight line at Tengah in Singapore, during 1963. The Canberra Mk.15 was a "tropicalized" Mk.6 fitted with underwing pylons for HE bombs or rocket packs, and provision for camera equipment. *(Photo: Jeff Thomas)*

Most Canberras assigned to the Near East Air Force were Mk.6 derivatives, particularly the B.Mk.6(BS) variant, as illustrated by WJ776 from No.139 Squadron. The sideways-looking Blue Shadow radar required the removal of the navigator's seat to make space for electronics. These aircraft were eventually modified to Mk.16 standard, with provision for a weapons pylon under each wing. Also visible in this photograph are the Canberra's lower airbrake fingers, in their extended position. *(Photo: Aeroplane)*

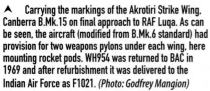

▲ Carrying the markings of the Akrotiri Strike Wing, Canberra B.Mk.15 on final approach to RAF Luqa. As can be seen, the aircraft (modified from B.Mk.6 standard) had provision for two weapons pylons under each wing, here mounting rocket pods. WH954 was returned to BAC in 1969 and after refurbishment it was delivered to the Indian Air Force as F1021. *(Photo: Godfrey Mangion)*

was now employing sub-contractors in much the same way as it had first developed as a sub-contractor company, many years previously. The first production B.Mk.6 made its first flight on 11 August 1953, followed by the initial Shorts-built example in October 1954. In July of that year the first B.Mk.6 was delivered to No.192 Squadron at Binbrook and by December the first examples of the B.Mk.6 were going to the Hemswell Wing, a

few miles to the west, followed by the arrival of two squadrons at Waddington. As the bomber force continued to build-up, the Canberra PR.Mk.3 received the improvements applied to the B.Mk.2, creating the PR.Mk.7. By the end of 1955, the RAF had a total of 37 operational Canberra squadrons, flying a mix of B.Mk.2 and B.Mk.6 bombers, PR.Mk.3 and PR.Mk.7 reconnaissance aircraft, and T.Mk.4 trainers, the latter mostly assigned to the OCU but with one or two being provided to each squadron for continuation training. This was in effect the peak of the Canberra's significance within Bomber Command and as the V-Force slowly began to emerge, the Canberra would gradually be replaced as a

high-altitude conventional bomber so that the new, nuclear strategic bombers could take over.

It was also at this stage that the Canberra's basic role was re-examined, as the RAF was now beginning to accept that the traditional concept of a fast, medium or high-altitude bomber might not necessarily be appropriated when the Soviet Union was rapidly developing interceptors and missiles that could reach the kind of altitudes that the RAF bombers had been cruising at. Height no longer meant safety and both the Canberras and the new V-Force would eventually abandon the quest for altitude and embrace low-level operations, among the hills and valleys at heights of 500ft or

During the winter of 1959-60 the Royal Aircraft Establishment and Institute of Aviation Medicine organized an investigation into sustained low-level, high-speed flight, using a fleet of Canberras drawn from No.231 OCU and RAF Upwood's Station Flight. These aircraft (WD950, WF890, WH648, WH664, WJ753 and WJ576) were fitted out with recording instrumentation and had their airframes strengthened for the trials. As "Swifter Flight" the aircraft were operated from Akrotiri, and some 1,000 hours of flying were conducted over ranges in Libya, some sorties involving sustained periods of flying at only 100ft above the desert floor. For the trials the aircraft received gloss white paint on their centre and forward fuselages and inner wing surfaces. After the trials were completed, some of the aircraft were withdrawn from use while WJ576, WF890 and WH664 were converted to T. Mk.17 standard and returned to RAF service.
(Photos: Tim McLelland collection)

much less. Down there 'in the weeds' it would be possible to hide from radar and much easier to evade enemy defences – at least for a little while longer than it would be high up in the stratosphere. The RAF concluded that the Canberra would be better suited to the low-level environment and with the V-Force slowly assuming the role of long range strategic bomber, the Canberra could now embrace the kind of role that it had really been designed for, supporting tactical operations at shorter ranges. It is worth noting that the Canberra had of course already become a rather different aircraft to the one that had been envisaged. When it was first ordered, the RAF had anticipated a bomber that would be smaller and lighter

Short Brothers was contracted to convert several Canberras into unmanned target drones, primarily for use by the Weapons Research Establishment (WRE), based at Woomera in Australia, in support of missile test programmes, including that for Bloodhound. The first conversion was Canberra U.Mk.10 WJ624, although the development of reliable control equipment became a protracted saga and the aircraft remained in the UK. Further conversions were produced for the Royal Navy, for use in trials of sea-launched missiles. WJ624 was also the first of these D.Mk.14s, developed from its original Mk.10 configuration with new internal equipment and servo-assisted flying controls as conceived for the PR.Mk.9. Most of the U.Mk.10 fleet was eventually destroyed through live missile firings in Australia, while the D.Mk.14s were primarily based at Hal Far, Malta, and destroyed by missiles fired from Royal Navy vessels. *(Photos: Tim McLelland collection)*

Canberra B.Mk.6 WH963 during 1966 in the markings of No.45 Squadron. The aircraft enjoyed a relatively straightforward service life, serving with Nos.12 and 45 Squadrons before being withdrawn in 1972. *(Photo: Tim McLelland collection)*

Manufactured as a Canberra B.Mk.6, WJ777 was reworked to B.Mk.6(BS) standard and eventually modified to B.Mk.16 configuration. It earned the distinction of becoming the very last Canberra assigned to the RAF's Near East Air Force and as such it received suitable markings on its nose section. BEA Vanguard (left) and Comet airliners are in the background of this shot at Hal Far, Malta. WJ777 ended its days on the fire dump at RAF Manston. *(Photo: Godfrey Mangion)*

Outwardly similar to the Canberra U.10 drone, B.Mk.2 WH967 was used as a trials aircraft for the B.Mk.15 and went to Boscombe Down for C9A clearance. It subsequently supported AS.30 missile development but crashed near Wheelus AB, Libya, during a June 1966 test flight. *(Photo: Tony Clarke collection)*

Canberra PR.Mk.7 WT523 was completed in May 1955 and immediately went to Germany, serving with Nos 31 and 17 Squadrons. It is shown in the latter's markings. The aircraft suffered a bird strike during a low-level sortie on 25 February 1971, and was subsequently withdrawn from use after a period in storage at Brüggen. It later became an airfield decoy at Laarbruch, where it was eventually scrapped. *(Photo: Tim McLelland collection)*

Here with the black and yellow star emblem of No.31 Squadron on its tail, Canberra PR.Mk.7 WT513 was completed at Samlesbury in January 1955. It was assigned to RAF Germany and served with Nos.31 and 17 Squadrons before being withdrawn in 1970. Like many of its contemporaries, it ended its days as an airfield decoy at Laarbruch. *(Photo: Tim McLelland collection)*

than the projected "strategic" V-Bombers that were to follow, with a shorter range but a faster speed. But as former Vice Chief of the Air Staff Sir Ralph Cochrane commented: "There was a tendency to look upon the Canberra as a long-range, high-flying bomber, and to press for equipment to enable it to undertake this role. At the end

however, it was generally accepted that the Canberra is a short range tactical bomber, that there is no equipment that will enable it to hit a small target from 45,000ft, and that it must therefore come down to a height from which it can achieve results." This effectively required the Canberra B.Mk.2 to abandon the notion of cruising at 40,000ft (with a ceiling

of 50,000ft), and shift to operational heights of 15-20,000ft and a ceiling of 40,000ft. Likewise, the envisaged 10,000lb bomb load would be reduced to a maximum of 8,000lb. Essentially, this meant an aircraft with more modest performance, but one much closer to English Electric's original proposal to create a direct replacement for the Mosquito. ❖

Canberra PR.Mk.7 WT521 was delivered to the RAF in May 1955. After a brief spell in storage it was assigned to RAF Germany and went on to serve with Nos 80 and 31 Squadrons. It is pictured shortly before its retirement, wearing the markings of No.31 Squadron on its tail and nose. WT521 was withdrawn in March 1971 and went to Wildenrath as an airfield decoy. *(Photo: Tim McLelland collection)*

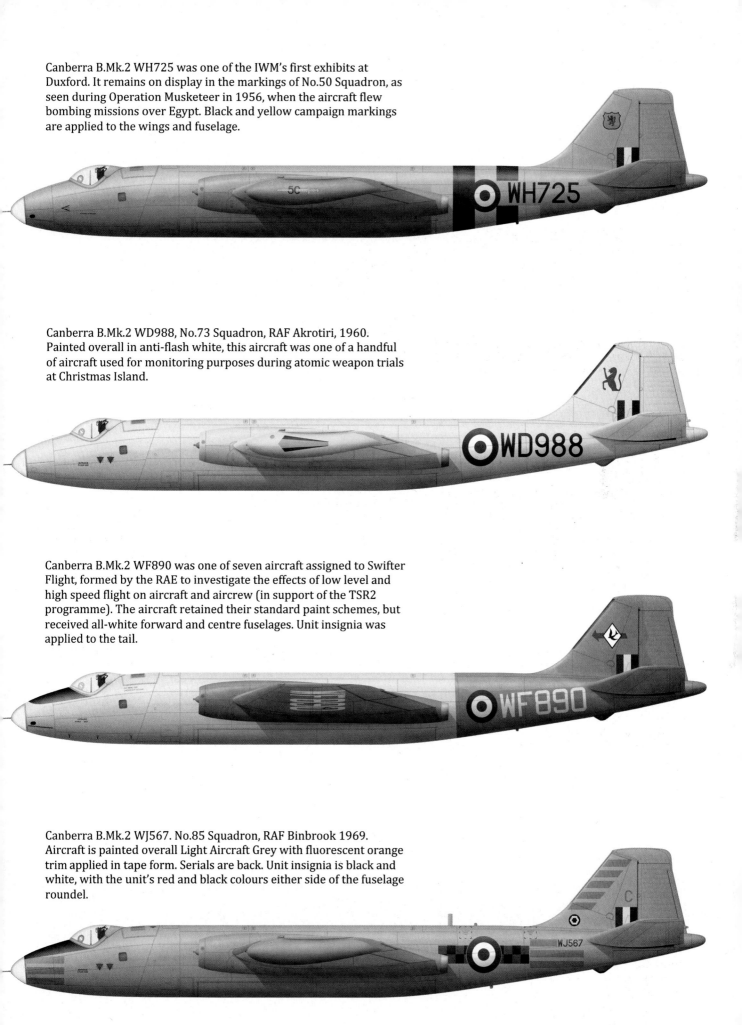

Canberra B.Mk.2 WH725 was one of the IWM's first exhibits at Duxford. It remains on display in the markings of No.50 Squadron, as seen during Operation Musketeer in 1956, when the aircraft flew bombing missions over Egypt. Black and yellow campaign markings are applied to the wings and fuselage.

Canberra B.Mk.2 WD988, No.73 Squadron, RAF Akrotiri, 1960. Painted overall in anti-flash white, this aircraft was one of a handful of aircraft used for monitoring purposes during atomic weapon trials at Christmas Island.

Canberra B.Mk.2 WF890 was one of seven aircraft assigned to Swifter Flight, formed by the RAE to investigate the effects of low level and high speed flight on aircraft and aircrew (in support of the TSR2 programme). The aircraft retained their standard paint schemes, but received all-white forward and centre fuselages. Unit insignia was applied to the tail.

Canberra B.Mk.2 WJ567. No.85 Squadron, RAF Binbrook 1969. Aircraft is painted overall Light Aircraft Grey with fluorescent orange trim applied in tape form. Serials are back. Unit insignia is black and white, with the unit's red and black colours either side of the fuselage roundel.

Drawings by Chris Sandham-Bailey (www.inkworm.co.uk)

CANBERRA CONSTRUCTION

A detailed look at the Canberra's design both inside and out

Britain's first jet bomber was born at an important period in the nation's aerospace history when both design and manufacturing capabilities were changing rapidly. The long years of World War Two were over, but the Canberra embraced technology that was clearly drawn from past experience. At the same time it also incorporated a great deal of modernity, not least in the employment of jet engines and in many other significant areas.

The Canberra was designed as a singularly clean aircraft from an aerodynamic viewpoint, and the targets aimed at by Petter when he roughed-out the basic design were sufficiently modest for it to be capable of manufacture along traditional lines. It was, for example, possible to employ quite conventional constant-thickness metal sheet throughout the skinning, and heavy forgings and machined members were conspicuous by their absence, except in such obvious places as the undercarriage attachments and wing-root joints. It followed that the airframe weight was substantially lower than that of similarly sized aircraft of later and faster design, and this fact, allied with the generous wing area of almost 1,000sq ft, endowed the aircraft with quite remarkable flying qualities. In fact, bearing in mind the aggregate engine thrust of some 15,000lb, the manoeuvrability and altitude performance of the Canberra were nothing short of remarkable. These notable aspects of performance were further improved in the largely redesigned Mk.9, created for the high altitude photographic reconnaissance role. All other Canberras shared essentially the same airframe. For example, the fuselage was of substantially circular section throughout its length and was assembled from standard frames and longitudinal components. Transport joints were provided to divide the structure into three roughly equal portions. The front fuselage incorporated the pressurised cockpit, bounded at the rear by a flat pressure bulkhead mounted at an oblique angle, and bearing the rails for the pilot's ejection seat. The crew entrance door was positioned near to the nose, forward of the cockpit canopy, on the starboard side. It opened outwards and upwards as a single unit, being hinged along its upper edge; a powered windbreak mounted immediately ahead of the door provided a dead-air region allowing the navigator to abandon the aircraft in an emergency – there was no ejection seat for him. In all British-built Canberras the pilot was seated on the port side. Early versions of the aircraft featured a large symmetrical cut-out above this region, sealed by a clear circular canopy of blown Perspex, but later ones (beginning with the Mk.8) employed a fighter-type canopy offset to port in line with the pilot's seat. This canopy did not open,

◄ Canberra B.Mk.2 WJ992 was converted to T.Mk.4 standard after completion. It was first assigned to Martlesham Heath and subsequently operated with the RAE and BLEU (Blind Landing Experimental Unit)) before joining the Royal Radar Establishment at Pershore. It then moved to RAE Bedford and remained there until April 1993 when it was retired. (Photo: FAST Museum)

A rare factory image of a Rolls-Royce Avon being lowered into position in the Canberra's wing. (Photo: Aeroplane)

Photographs taken at the Samlesbury Canberra production facility show the aircraft's tail section, engine installation, wing and forward fuselage structure.
(Photos: Aeroplane)

The Canberra B.Mk.2's
engine nacelle viewed up
close with panels removed
for engineering access.
(Photos: Tim McLelland
collection)

Canberra B.Mk.2

(Drawings from Tim McLelland collection)

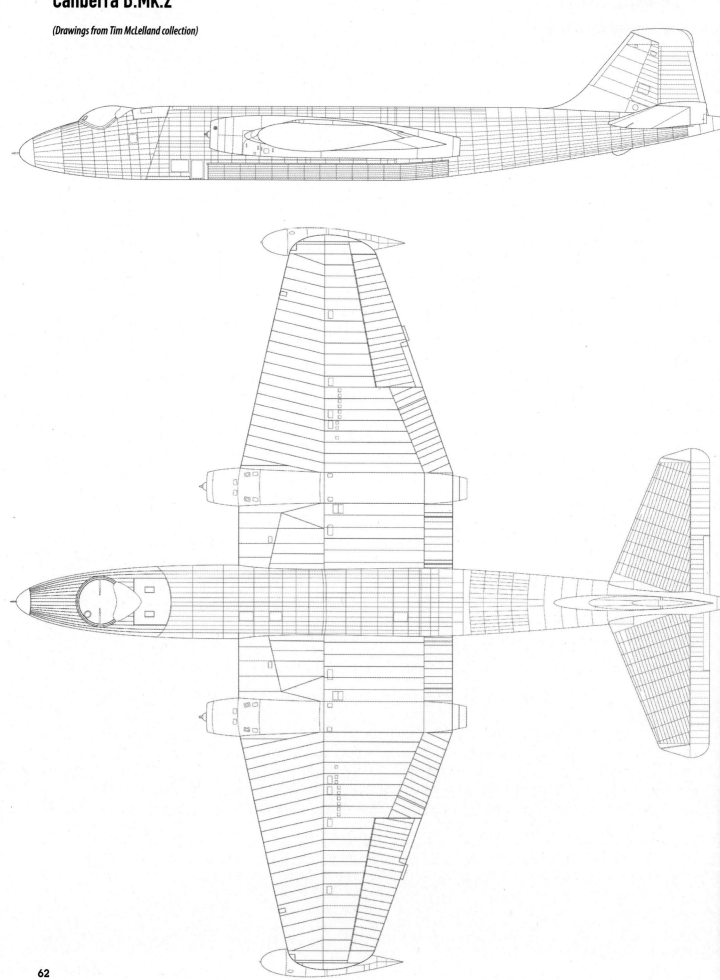

Canberra B.Mk.6

(Drawings from Tim McLelland collection)

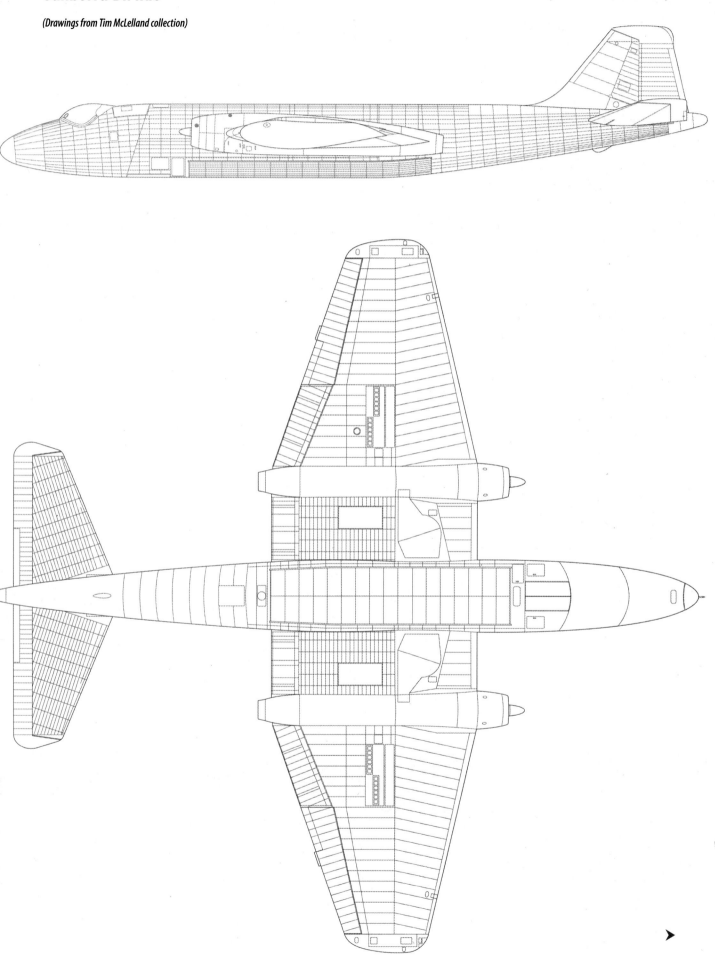

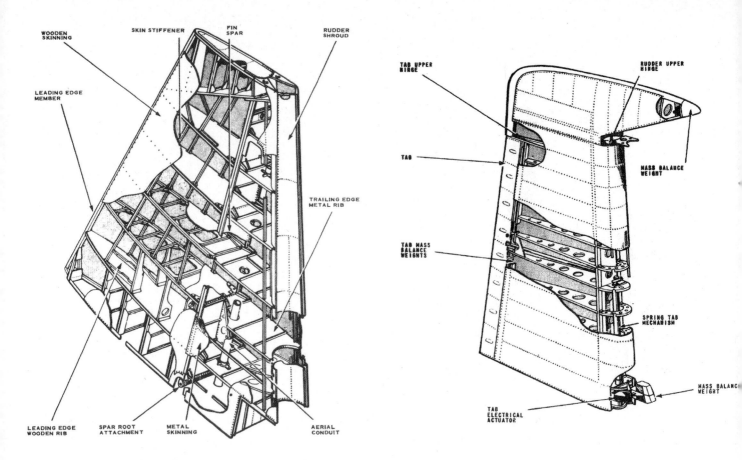

WOODEN SKINNING
SKIN STIFFENER
FIN SPAR
RUDDER SHROUD
LEADING EDGE MEMBER
TRAILING EDGE METAL RIB
LEADING EDGE WOODEN RIB
SPAR ROOT ATTACHMENT
METAL SKINNING
AERIAL CONDUIT

TAB UPPER HINGE
RUDDER UPPER HINGE
TAB
MASS BALANCE WEIGHT
TAB MASS BALANCE WEIGHTS
SPRING TAB MECHANISM
TAB ELECTRICAL ACTUATOR
MASS BALANCE WEIGHT

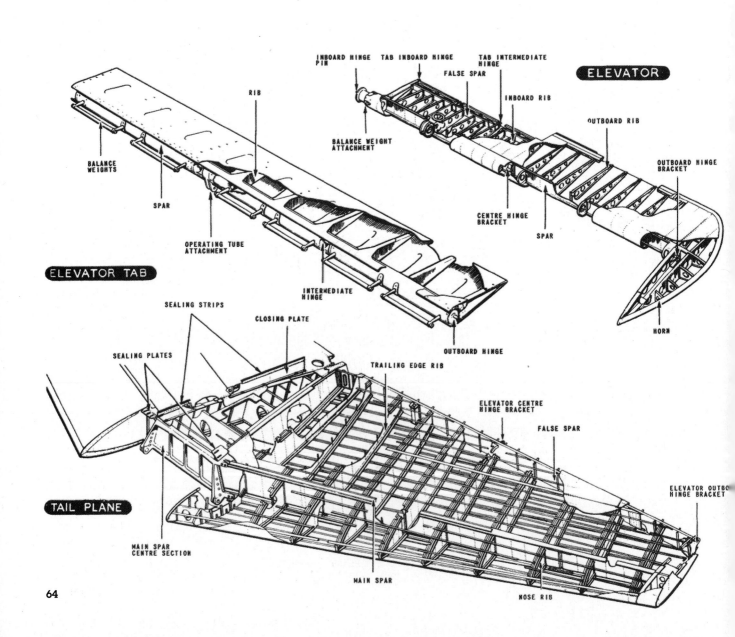

INBOARD HINGE PIN
TAB INBOARD HINGE
TAB INTERMEDIATE HINGE
FALSE SPAR
ELEVATOR
BALANCE WEIGHT ATTACHMENT
INBOARD RIB
OUTBOARD RIB
OUTBOARD HINGE BRACKET
RIB
BALANCE WEIGHTS
SPAR
OPERATING TUBE ATTACHMENT
CENTRE HINGE BRACKET
SPAR
ELEVATOR TAB
INTERMEDIATE HINGE
HORN
OUTBOARD HINGE
SEALING STRIPS
CLOSING PLATE
TRAILING EDGE RIB
ELEVATOR CENTRE HINGE BRACKET
FALSE SPAR
SEALING PLATES
ELEVATOR OUTBOARD HINGE BRACKET
TAIL PLANE
MAIN SPAR CENTRE SECTION
MAIN SPAR
NOSE RIB

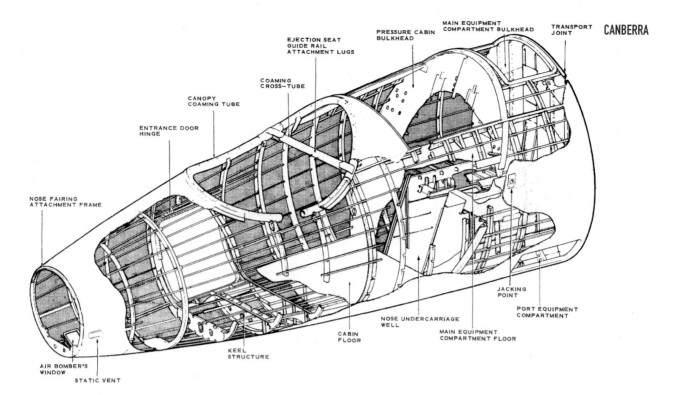

NOSE FAIRING
ATTACHMENT FRAME

ENTRANCE DOOR
HINGE

CANOPY
COAMING TUBE

COAMING
CROSS-TUBE

EJECTION SEAT
GUIDE RAIL
ATTACHMENT LUGS

PRESSURE CABIN
BULKHEAD

MAIN EQUIPMENT
COMPARTMENT BULKHEAD

TRANSPORT
JOINT

AIR BOMBER'S
WINDOW

STATIC VENT

KEEL
STRUCTURE

CABIN
FLOOR

NOSE UNDERCARRIAGE
WELL

MAIN EQUIPMENT
COMPARTMENT FLOOR

JACKING
POINT

PORT EQUIPMENT
COMPARTMENT

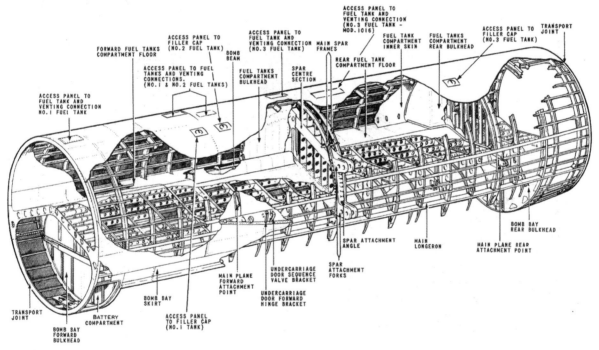

ACCESS PANEL TO
FUEL TANK AND
VENTING CONNECTION
(NO.3 FUEL TANK –
MOD.1016)

FORWARD FUEL TANKS
COMPARTMENT FLOOR

ACCESS PANEL TO
FILLER CAP
(NO.2 FUEL TANK)

ACCESS PANEL TO
FUEL TANK AND
VENTING CONNECTION
(NO.3 FUEL TANK)

MAIN SPAR
FRAMES

FUEL TANK
COMPARTMENT
INNER SKIN

FUEL TANKS
COMPARTMENT
REAR BULKHEAD

ACCESS PANEL TO
FILLER CAP
(NO.3 FUEL TANK)

TRANSPORT
JOINT

BOMB
BEAM

ACCESS PANEL TO FUEL
TANKS AND VENTING
CONNECTIONS.
(NO.1 & NO.2 FUEL TANKS)

FUEL TANKS
COMPARTMENT
BULKHEAD

SPAR
CENTRE
SECTION

REAR FUEL TANK
COMPARTMENT FLOOR

ACCESS PANEL TO
FUEL TANK AND
VENTING CONNECTION
NO.1 FUEL TANK

BOMB BAY
REAR BULKHEAD

MAIN PLANE REAR
ATTACHMENT POINT

SPAR ATTACHMENT
ANGLE

MAIN
LONGERON

MAIN PLANE
FORWARD
ATTACHMENT
POINT

UNDERCARRIAGE
DOOR SEQUENCE
VALVE BRACKET

SPAR
ATTACHMENT
FORKS

TRANSPORT
JOINT

BOMB BAY
SKIRT

UNDERCARRIAGE
DOOR FORWARD
HINGE BRACKET

BATTERY
COMPARTMENT

ACCESS PANEL
TO FILLER CAP
(NO.1 TANK)

BOMB BAY
FORWARD
BULKHEAD

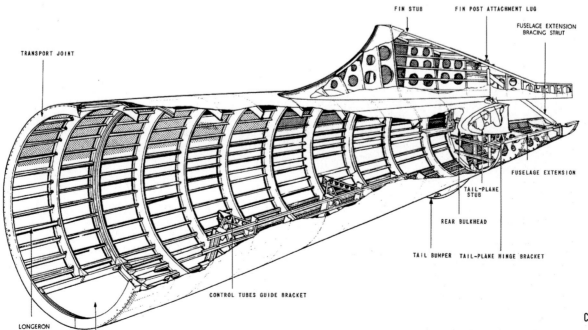

FIN STUB

FIN POST ATTACHMENT LUG

FUSELAGE EXTENSION
BRACING STRUT

TRANSPORT JOINT

FUSELAGE EXTENSION

TAIL-PLANE
STUB

REAR BULKHEAD

TAIL BUMPER

TAIL-PLANE HINGE BRACKET

CONTROL TUBES GUIDE BRACKET

LONGERON

REAR ACCESS HATCH

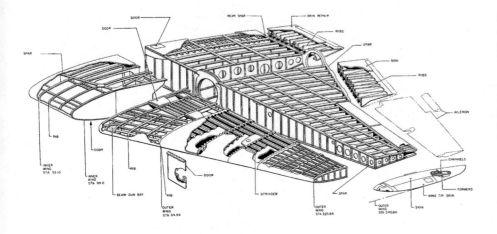

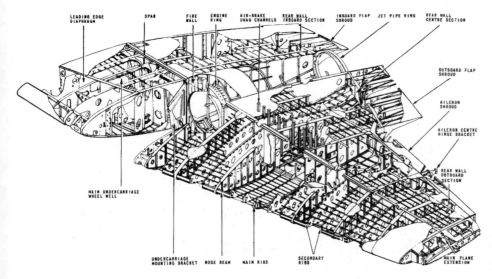

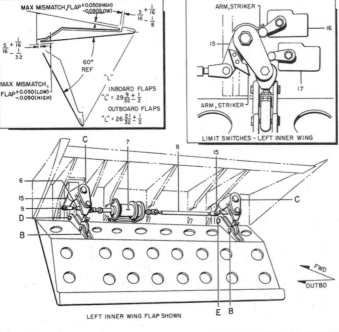

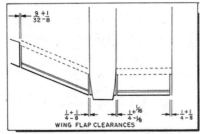

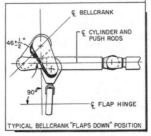

WING FLAP CLEARANCES

TYPICAL BELLCRANK "FLAPS DOWN" POSITION

but it could be jettisoned if necessary by ten explosive bolts, and in dire emergency the pilot could fire his Mk.1C ejection seat through the canopy itself.

Of almost uniform cross-section, the centre fuselage extended from frames 12 to 31. Two heavy frames at station 21 were aligned with the main wing spar, and were separated by the spar centre-section forging which had attachment forks projecting on each side of the aircraft. Throughout the length of the centre fuselage, provision was made for a bomb bay on the underside and fuel cells above, the two being separated by a strong floor structure of double-skinned construction. Each bomb door was supported on forged brackets at its ends and by rollers operating in the channelled ends of the transverse fuselage frames at seven stations along the bomb bay. The Mk.8 aircraft could be fitted with a gun pack (as could interdictor versions of the Mk.6) by removing the bomb doors and installing flare-bay doors ahead of the pack and making other small modifications. The rear fuselage was manufactured along conventional construction lines. It incorporated the stubs of the fin and tailplanes, and an extension at its rear end terminated in a dielectric cap associated with internal electronic equipment.

Aerodynamically related to that of the Meteor, the wing was completely unswept, and outboard of the engine nacelles, it tapered sharply from the considerable root chord of 19ft. Port and starboard main planes were built separately and were attached to anchorages projecting from strong bridge-pieces within the fuselage. Wing bending loads were absorbed principally by the single main wing spar at about 40 per cent chord. This spar was a built-up beam with a plate web and machined alloy booms, the section of which changed from a plain T at the tip to a complex T-like form at the root. Around the engine jet pipe the spar loads were transmitted by the booms (which were unbroken) and by massive forged light-alloy ring-members, ahead of which was a heat-resistant steel fire wall. The main wing box was completed by what was termed as the rear wall, consisting of a span-wise web ahead of the flaps and ailerons and connected across the jet-pipe cutout by a forged I-section ring. The remaining structure of sheet ribs and bulb-angle span-wise stringers was also of conventional design. The complete assembly was skinned with constant-thickness sheet, flush-riveted throughout and with butt-joints reinforced by doubler strips.

Like the wing, the tailplane featured a single spar positioned well forward and a false spar at the trailing edge of the main box (although, unlike the wing, this rearmost member could run straight from root to tip). Port and starboard tailplanes were joined by transverse bridge pieces lying within the fuselage. The bridge piece, or 'centre section' for the main spar was a forged light-alloy member, on the forward face of which were a

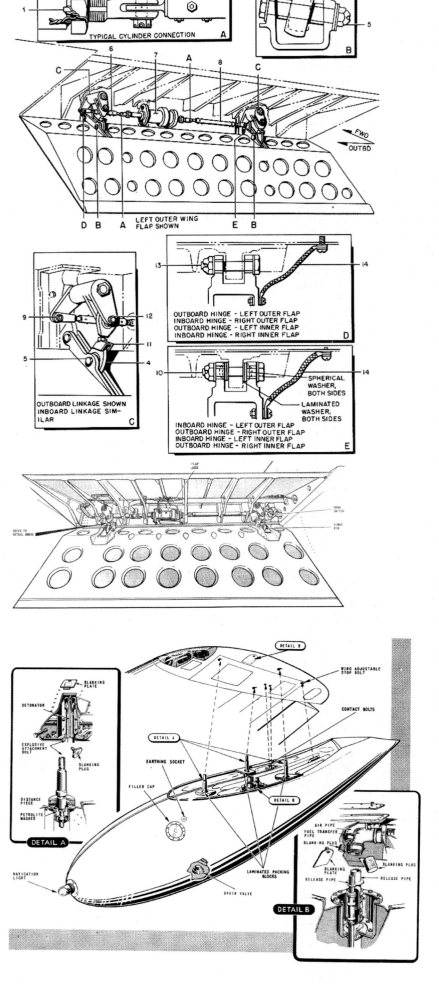

pair of trunnions upon which the tailplane was pivoted to the rear of fuselage frame 42. Near the false rear spar was an anchorage for an English Electric actuator with which the tailplane incidence could be varied. The fin likewise had a single spar, but the structure was otherwise most unconventional; unusually, the leading-edge portion (back to some 60 per cent chord) comprised wooden ribs, a leading-edge member of laminated spruce and a plywood skin. The rearmost edges of the skin were Reduxed (glued) to the T-section booms on the forward face of the spar. All the control surfaces were of conventional construction, with single spars, pressed-sheet ribs and light-gauge skinning behind a D-section nose. The ailerons had inset hinges and were balanced by an aerodynamic beak (with critical clearances) and adjustable strips of heavy alloy. The elevators had large horn balances and mass balances carried on tubular arms while the rudder had a similar system supplemented by a second mass-balance weight in the tip of the horn. Both ailerons were fitted with conventional spring tabs, and similar surfaces were also carried by both elevators and the rudder. All control circuits were operated through push/pull tubes from pedals and a 'spectacle' stick in the cockpit. For trimming purposes, the tailplane-actuator switch was located close to the pilot's thumb. Lateral trim was accomplished by a biassing circuit, controlled by an electric actuator, at the base of the control column. For asymmetric flying the rudder tab could be offset by an ad hoc actuator, which positioned the outer spring-tab torque tube. In addition, the starboard elevator tab could be adjusted on the ground for trimming purposes.

For emergency purposes, a control-column snatch unit was fitted. Should the pilot wish to leave the aircraft by means of his ejection seat, he could, by pulling the screened snatch-unit handle on the control panel, sever the elevator control and release a powerful spring, which pulled the control column forward against the instrument panel. This provided the pilot with an unobstructed escape path.

Split flaps were fitted in four portions beneath the wings. Each surface was a very simple triangular section structure with a single pressed spar and an upper skin liberally provided with flanged lightening holes. Each of the four sections was hung on two hinges and was operated through a bell-crank linkage by a single hydraulic jack behind the rear wall of the wing, which operated through span-wise push-pull rods. The airbrakes were less conventional, and comprised 21 drag channels disposed vertically within each wing behind the main spar. When the brakes were closed, the ends of the channels laid flush with the surface of the wing. They could be made to project a considerable distance into the airstream through an assemblage of rocker arms on a torque tube, which was pivoted by a hydraulic jack anchored to the rear wall. Twelve of the channels projected beneath the wing and nine above.

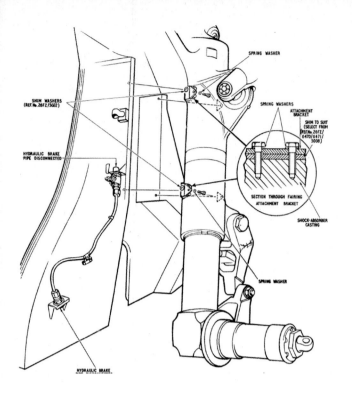

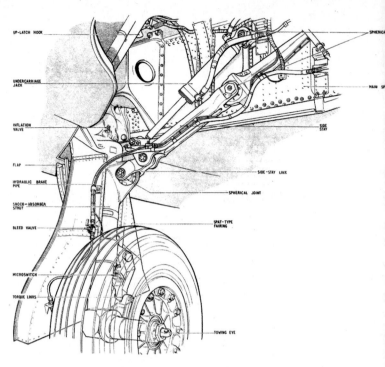

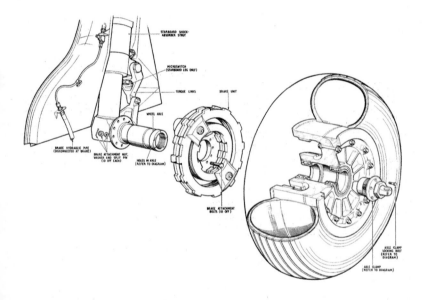

Design and manufacture of the main undercarriage units was handled by English Electric. Each unit comprised a single forged light-alloy leg containing an oleo-pneumatic strut inflated to about 400psi. The tyres, wheels and plate brakes were all manufactured by Dunlop, and the units retracted inwards into the wing under the pull of a hydraulic jack. The nose gear assembly was mounted well aft, actually being attached to a pair of forged brackets on the rear face of the pressure bulkhead. The leg itself was a levered suspension, liquid spring product of Dowty Equipment, and it carried twin Dunlop wheel units, each provided with a mudguard. The complete assembly was hydraulically retracted to the rear and the wheels were fully castering, with a spring-loaded centring mechanism that damped potential shimmying, and centred the wheels for retraction. A rubber-shod tail bumper was fitted beneath the rear fuselage.

The powerplant of all British production Canberras comprised a pair of Rolls-Royce Avon turbojets. The precise type of Avon fitted to any given mark of Canberra varied, but aircraft within the 'first generation' of Canberra derivatives all employed engines in the Avon 100 series. Each engine was carried on four self-aligning mountings. The rear mounts were spherically-radiused collars fitted to trunnions bolted to either side of the engine node box. The collars were located between bearing-blocks bolted directly to the inboard and outboard engine ribs. Corresponding anchorages were bolted to the extreme forward end of the engine ribs; each carried a cup bracket within which was a ball socket on the end of a tie-rod from which was suspended the adjacent front mounting of the engine on the lower part of the compressor casing. From the engine exhaust cone a transition piece, secured by a clamping ring, led to the jet pipe proper which passed through the

wing spar banjo and through the forged ring in the rear wall of the wing box. At its forward end each jet pipe was bolted to the transition piece and was also supported by a pair of lugs resting on channel-section runners which formed part of the wing structure. At the rear, the pipe was provided with a housing bracket on either side which located an eccentric spigot in the rear-wall ring; the latter allowed the pipe to expand axially and provided for vertical alignment on installation. Access to the complete engine was available by the removal of four panels. Much the largest was the front cowl, which encircled the complete engine and was removed in a forwards direction. Beneath the wing leading edge was a semi-circular service panel, and the run of the jet pipe was covered by upper and lower rear cowls. All these portions were attached to each other or to the wing by Dzus fasteners and toggle latches. Most of the 100-series Avons installed in early Canberras

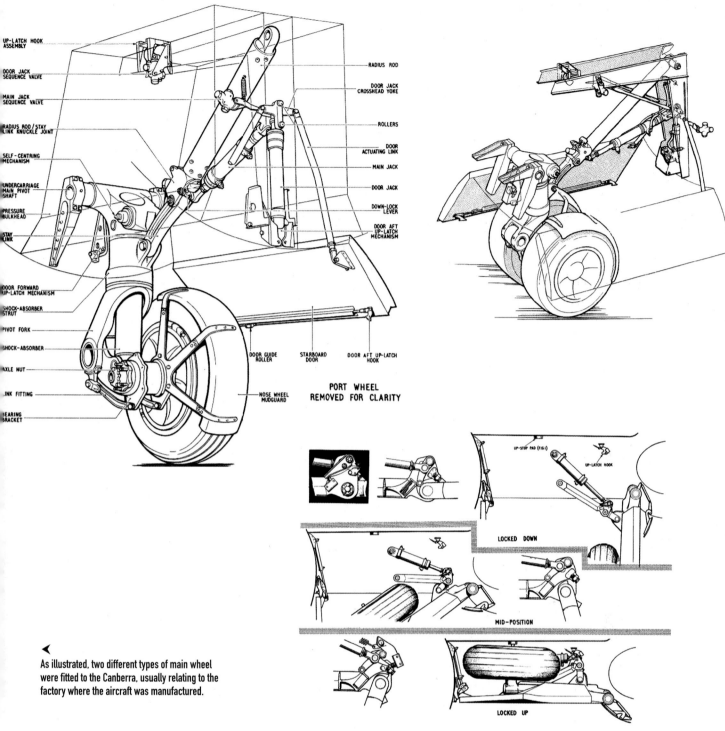

UP-LATCH HOOK ASSEMBLY
DOOR JACK SEQUENCE VALVE
MAIN JACK SEQUENCE VALVE
RADIUS ROD / STAY LINK KNUCKLE JOINT
SELF-CENTRING MECHANISM
UNDERCARRIAGE MAIN PIVOT SHAFT
PRESSURE BULKHEAD
STAY LINK
DOOR FORWARD UP-LATCH MECHANISM
SHOCK-ABSORBER STRUT
PIVOT FORK
SHOCK-ABSORBER
AXLE NUT
LINK FITTING
BEARING BRACKET

RADIUS ROD
DOOR JACK CROSSHEAD YOKE
ROLLERS
DOOR ACTUATING LINK
MAIN JACK
DOOR JACK
DOWN-LOCK LEVER
DOOR AFT UP-LATCH MECHANISM

DOOR GUIDE ROLLER
STARBOARD DOOR
DOOR AFT UP-LATCH HOOK
NOSE WHEEL MUDGUARD

PORT WHEEL
REMOVED FOR CLARITY

UP-STOP PAD (FIG I)
UP-LATCH HOOK
LOCKED DOWN
MID-POSITION
LOCKED UP

◄

As illustrated, two different types of main wheel were fitted to the Canberra, usually relating to the factory where the aircraft was manufactured.

were the RA.7 or RA.21 (7,500/8,000lb) although the first production aircraft employed the 6,500lb thrust RA.3, which was also fitted to the Canberra T.Mk.4 trainer. These early engines generally had single-breech turbo-starters mounted within the streamlined bullet in the centre of the air intake. The later engines, such as those fitted to the B.Mk.6 and B(I).Mk.8 had a triple-breech starter which gave rise to a longer bullet that projected well ahead of the intake lip. Exhaust from the starter was discharged to atmosphere through a radial duct across the intake, terminating in a flush vent in the outer skin of the front cowl. The lubrication system, using OX-38 (OX-11 on earlier aircraft) oil, was self-contained within each engine, oil cooling being effected by a heat exchanger through which was passed oil and high-pressure fuel. Each Avon wheel case drove an extension shaft coupled to a Rotol accessory gearbox within the wing on the inboard side of the jet pipe.

The majority of the Canberra's internal fuel capacity was located in three tanks in the upper part of the fuselage above the bomb bay. The forward and centre tanks were flexible self-sealing cells with internal bracing while the rearmost tank was a crash-proof collapsible bag. In certain types of Canberra (including the PR.Mk.7 and B.Mk.8) additional internal fuel was carried within the wings, giving a substantial increase in range. All marks of Canberra were cleared to carry jettisonable streamlined tanks beneath the wing tips, each with a capacity of 244 Imp. gal. SBAC flush fillers were provided in the top decking of the fuselage for gravity filling, and late-model Canberras, including the Mk.8, had additional fillers in the wings. Three methyl bromide extinguisher bottles provided fire protection, two serving the engines and one the fuselage tanks and bomb bay.

Pressurisation of the crew compartment was effected by air bled from the Avon

compressors. The hot bleed air was controlled by Teddington gate valves and taken into a common duct between the power plants. Hot air was fed directly to cameras, the gun-pack and other operational equipment, while the major proportion was passed through primary and secondary coolers in the wing leading edges and through a Godfrey cold-air unit. Finally, supplies of hot and cold air were fed to a two-way mixing valve giving air of the required temperature and quality for the cabin. The air was passed through a water extractor and individual supplies were provided for each crew member and for canopy and bombing panel demisting.

Electrical power was generated and distributed at a nominal voltage of 24/27.5 using a single-pole DC system. The system was energised by a pair of 9kW Type 512 generators operating in parallel and driven off the accessory gearbox inboard of the engines. Rotary inverters provided supplies ➤

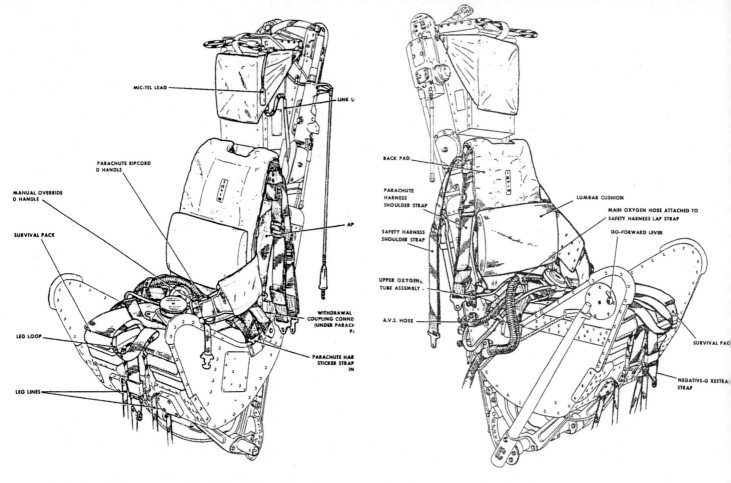

MIC-TEL LEAD

LINK L

PARACHUTE RIPCORD
D HANDLE

MANUAL OVERRIDE
D HANDLE

SURVIVAL PACK

AP

LEG LOOP

WITHDRAWAL
COUPLING CONNE
(UNDER PARACH
PJ

LEG LINES

PARACHUTE HAR
STICKER STRAP
IN

BACK PAD

PARACHUTE
HARNESS
SHOULDER STRAP

LUMBAR CUSHION

MAIN OXYGEN HOSE ATTACHED TO
SAFETY HARNESS LAP STRAP

SAFETY HARNESS
SHOULDER STRAP

GO-FORWARD LEVER

UPPER OXYGEN
TUBE ASSEMBLY

A.V.S. HOSE

SURVIVAL PAC

NEGATIVE-G RESTRA
STRAP

Although various ejection seat types were installed in the Canberra, the standard seat fitted to most variants was the Martin–Baker Type 2CS. *(Drawings courtesy Martin-Baker)*

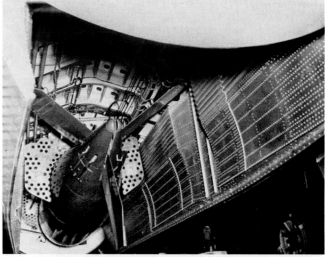

External and internal stores, clockwise from above left: A SNEB rocket pod, Mk.7 nuclear bomb inside the bomb bay, the Rushton target pod (with banner pods attached), and Stilletto high-speed target. A 2in rocket pod is shown at right.
(Photos: Tim McLelland collection & FAST Museum)

of 400Hz three-phase and 1,600Hz single-phase current for instruments and electronics.

Each of the two accessory gearboxes drove a Lockheed Mk.7 hydraulic pump which energised the hydraulic system to 2,700/ 3,000psi. The system served undercarriage retraction, flaps, air brakes, bomb doors and wheel brakes. OM-15 fluid (mineral-based) was employed, the reservoir being located on frame 12 at the extreme rear of the front fuselage. A small self-contained system could be energised by an air bottle, to operate the windbreak door already mentioned.

In the Mk.8 Canberra, oxygen for the crew was carried in a gaseous form in two cylinders each of 2,550-litre capacity and two of 750-litre capacity. All four bottles were mounted in the equipment compartment behind the pressure bulkhead; the cylinders were arranged in isolated pairs, the high-pressure circuit being duplicated.

Most Canberras were fitted with TR 1985 or TR1986 VHF communications radio, the sets themselves being mounted immediately behind the pressure bulkhead on the port side of the fuselage and the associated whip aerials being mounted above the fuselage on the centreline. A conventional system was fitted, the equipment being mounted beneath the pilot's floor and the aerials comprising a marker aerial in the starboard main wheel bay, a glide-path aerial in the outer starboard wing leading edge and a localiser aerial in the outer port wing leading edge. When a radio altimeter was fitted, two dipole aerials were provided for the system on the underside of the rear fuselage. Should Gee be fitted, the system was served by an L-shaped wire mesh aerial mounted within the wooden structure of the fin.

This description applies to what was arguably the most important mark of Canberra to be produced, 'the Mk.8'. Owing to its remarkable versatility the Mk.8 superseded some earlier single-purpose Canberras in RAF service, and it was also employed by the air forces of India, Venezuela, Peru, and New Zealand. Numerous Mk.6 bombers in RAF service were also converted to the B(I).MK.6 standard by making provision to carry under wing stores and a bomb bay gun pack. Weapons system equipment carried by the Canberra varied between each variant, depending on the role in which the aircraft was operating, and a great deal of equipment differed, according to the sub-type of aircraft concerned. Canberras employed in bomber roles by the Royal Air Force were of course capable of carrying kiloton-yield nuclear stores, primarily in the weapons provided by the United States, or the British Red Beard tactical bomb. A very wide range of conventional stores could be accommodated, including six 1,000lb bombs or mines of various types, or a pair of Mk.2 triple carriers (which were specially designed for the Canberra by Avro). Three triple carriers could be used to accommodate six 800lb clusters of incendiaries or 18 100lb practice bombs. Aft of the main spar on each outer wing on some variants a single pylon was provided for a stores load of 1,000lb.

Visual bombing could be conducted from a prone position in the nose, and more sophisticated means of delivery — including automatic LABS (Low Altitude Bombing System) — were also possible. When operating in the interdictor role, the secondary bomb beams were removed to enable a large gun pack to be accommodated in the rear part of the weapons bay. This pack housed four 20mm Hispano guns. Provision was made for the carriage of a very great quantity of ammunition (sufficient for 55 seconds of continuous firing) and the pack was provided with full heating and gas purging systems. Associated with the pack was a G45B cine camera, which was mounted in the inner starboard wing leading edge. When the pack was installed, the forward part of the bomb bay could be used to house sixteen 4.5in flares or a single Avro triple carrier upon which three 1,000lb stores could be mounted. ❖

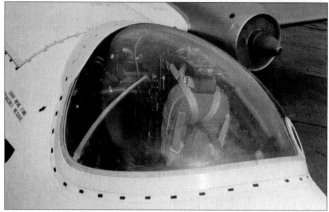

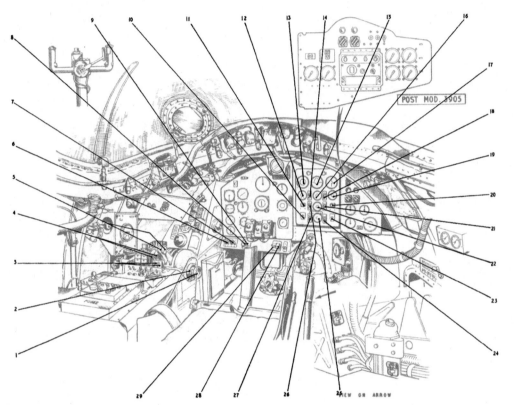

1	FRICTION DAMPER, H.P. FUEL SHUT-OFF COCK LEVERS
2	FRICTION DAMPER, THROTTLE CONTROL LEVERS
3	FUEL PUMP ISOLATION SWITCHES
4	ENGINE RE-LIGHT SWITCHES
5	THROTTLE CONTROL LEVERS
6	NO.1 ENGINE MASTER STARTING SWITCH
7	NO.2 ENGINE MASTER STARTING SWITCH
8	STARTER PUSH SWITCH, PORT ENGINE
9	IGNITION SWITCH, PORT ENGINE
10	BOMB BAY FUEL TANK PORT SWITCH (POST MOD.1490) OR SWITCH SETTING LABEL (POST MOD.2712)
11	FUEL PRESSURE WARNING LIGHT
12	OIL PRESSURE GAUGE, PORT ENGINE
13	ENGINE SPEED INDICATOR, PORT ENGINE
14	FUEL COCK AND PUMP SWITCH, NO.1 TANK, PORT ENGINE
15	JET PIPE TEMPERATURE INDICATOR
16	FUEL CONTENTS GAUGE, NO.1 TANK
17	ENGINE SPEED INDICATOR, STARBOARD ENGINE
18	FUEL COCK AND PUMP SWITCH, NO.1 TANK STARBOARD ENGINE
19	OIL PRESSURE GAUGE, STARBOARD ENGINE
20	FUEL PRESSURE WARNING LIGHT, STARBOARD ENGINE
21	FUEL COCK AND PUMP SWITCH, NO.2 TANK, STARBOARD ENGINE
22	FUEL CONTENTS GAUGE, NO.2 TANK
23	BOMB BAY FUEL TANK, STARBOARD SWITCH (POST MOD.1490)
24	FUEL COCK AND PUMP SWITCH, NO.3 TANK, STARBOARD ENGINE
25	FUEL CONTENTS GAUGE, NO.3 TANK
26	FUEL COCK AND PUMP SWITCH, NO.2 TANK, PORT ENGINE
27	FUEL COCK AND PUMP SWITCH, NO.3 TANK, PORT ENGINE
28	STARTER PUSH SWITCH, STARBOARD ENGINE
29	IGNITION SWITCH, STARBOARD ENGINE

POST MOD. 3905

VIEW ON ARROW

Fig. 2. Engine controls and instruments

Cockpit layout key

Electrical control panel

1. No.5 Inverter STOP push-button.
2. No.5 Inverter START push-button.
3. No.4 / No. 5 inverter changeover switch.
4. No.4 inverter switch.
5. Circuit breakers - from left to right - Pilot's services, No.1 generator, No.2 generator.
6. No.1 generator failure warning light.
7. No.1 generator switch - port.
8. Battery isolation switch.
9. No.2 generator failure warning light.
10. No.2 generator switch - starboard.
11. Circuit breakers - from left to right - No.1 tank starboard pump, No.1 tank starboard cock, No.1 tank port pump, No.1 tank port cock.

12. Harness release lever.
13. Thigh guard clamp.
14. Seat adjusting lever.
15. Hydraulic hand pump.
16. Oxygen selector valve.
17. Oxygen emergency supply control.
18. Circuit breakers - from left to right - No 3 tank starboard pump, No.3 tank starboard cock, No. 3 tank port pump, No.3 tank port cock.
19. Circuit breakers - from left to right - No.2 tank starboard pump, No.2 tank starboard cock, No.2 tank port pump, No.2 tank port cock.
20. Gee H supply switch.
21. Tail warning device supply switch.
22. Rebecca supply switch.

Fig 2. Cockpit Port side

23. Fuel vent valve heater switch.
24. Direct Vision (DV) panel heater switch.

25. Pressure head heater switch.
26. Fuses in Gee circuit.
27. Bomb door control switch.
28. Bomb door warning lamp.
29. Emergency bomb jettison switch.
30. Emergency bomb selector lever.
31. Oxygen regulator.
32. HP fuel cock lever.
33. Intercom switches.
34. Throttle lever.
35. IFF receiver and G/D switches.
36. Canopy jettison and snatch unit master safety switch and canopy jettison switch (hidden by throttle levers).
37. Undercarriage emergency selector handle.
38. Flap selector switch lever.
39. Adjustable cold air vent.
40. Flap position indicator.
41. Throttle lever friction control.
42. HP fuel cock lever friction controls.
43. HP fuel pump isolating valve switches.
44. External light switches - from top to bottom -

COCKPIT—PORT SIDE

FIG 2

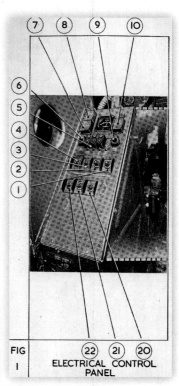

FIG 1

ELECTRICAL CONTROL PANEL

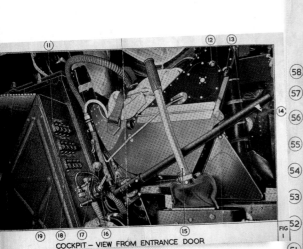

COCKPIT – VIEW FROM ENTRANCE DOOR

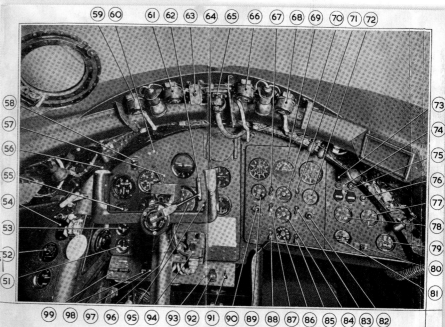

FIG 1

INSTRUMENT PANEL

navigation light switches, taxi light switches, landing lamp switches, identification lights switch, identification lights colour switch, external lights master switch.
45. Identification lights morsing push button.
46. Rudder trimming switch.
47. Aileron trimming switch.
48. Control column snatch unit operating lever.
49. Wing tip tanks jettison button.
50. Canopy 'sandwich' demister switch.

Fig 3. Cockpit – Instrument Panel

51. Aileron trim indicator.
52. Undercarriage position indicator.
53. Rudder trim indicator.
54. Undercarriage selector push-button.
55. Tailplane incidence indicator.
56. Bomb release push-button.
57. Air brake control switch.
58. Flight instruments emergency supply indicator.

59. Port UV lamp dimmer switch.
60. Gee-H indicator.
61. Port flood lamps dimmer switch.
62. Brake lever.
63. Emergency lamp switch.
64. Tailplane incidence control switch.
65. Magnetic stand-by compass.
66. Starboard flood lamps dimmer switch.
67. LP cock and booster pump switch - No.1 tank port.
68. Starboard UV lamps dimmer switch.
69. Duel jet pipe temperature gauge.
70. Fuel contents gauge - No.1 tank.
71. LP cock and booster pump switch - No.1 tank starboard.
72. Oil pressure gauge - starboard.
73. Cabin pressure warning horn override switch.
74. Engine fire-warning lights.
75. Engine fire extinguisher push-buttons.
76. Fuel bay fire warning light.
77. Hydraulic warning gauge.
78. Cabin altimeter.

79. Brake pressure gauge.
80. Cabin heating and pressure switch.
81. Cabin heating and pressurising indicator.
82. Fuel pressure warning light - starboard.
83. LP cock and booster pump switch - No.2 starboard.
84. Fuel contents gauge - No.2 tank.
85. LP cock and booster pump switch - No.3 starboard.
86. Fuel contents gauge - No.3 tank.
87. LP cock and booster pump switch - No.2 port.
88. L.P. cock and booster pump switch - No.3 port.
89. Oil pressure gauge - port.
90. Fuel pressure warning light.
91. Mk 4B compass changeover switch.
92. Starter push-button - starboard.
93. Ignition switch - starboard.
94. VHF channel selector and volume control.
95. VHF press-to-transmit push-button.
96. Mk 4B compass repeater.
97. Ignition switch - port.
98. Starter push-button - port.
99. Master starting switches.

INTRUDER INTERLUDE

The RAF's nuclear-capable Canberra Mk.8 interdictor

The erstwhile Canberra B.Mk.5 prototype, VX185 returned to the air in 1954 after conversion as the B(I).Mk.8 prototype. *(Photo: Aeroplane)*

Canberra production at Short's Belfast factory in 1954, with the first Mk.8 nearing completion. As with many Canberra contracts, the Mk.8 was outsourced to a sub-contractor to ease the burden on English Electric's Samlesbury factory, where work on the Canberra and Lightning was under way. *(Photo: Tim McLelland collection)*

During the first years of service with the RAF, the Canberra B.Mk.2 was still very much a 'traditional' medium level bomber, and it had been specifically designed to perform this task. It wasn't designed to operate at very low level, nor was it equipped to deliver anything other than conventional free-fall high explosive (HE) bombs, even if the knowledge of atomic weaponry had been in the minds of both the Air Staff and English Electric. If the Canberra was to be operated in the attack (or 'intruder') role, it would have to change quite considerably.

Rather than merely relying on modifications to the existing Canberra B.Mk.2 and B.Mk.6 bomber design, the RAF issued Operational Requirement OR.302, calling for a development of the standard Canberra model that would be suited to low level operations as an 'interdictor' bomber. The term 'interdictor' (or 'intruder' in American parlance) implied a ground attack capability and not only as a tactical bomber but as a more flexible attack aircraft, through the use of rockets or gun armament. English Electric proposed the conversion of the existing Canberra Mk.5 prototype that had been built in response to an Air Ministry requirement for a radar-equipped target marker aircraft. Without the original 'blind bomber' Canberra Mk.1 fitted with its own radar equipment, the Canberra Mk.2 was

reliant on visual conditions unless Gee cover was present - Gee was the wartime-vintage radio navigation system comprising locator beacons that enabled navigation through a triangulation technique. Bomber Command therefore specified that the Canberra's role was defined as being: "bombing in support of the land battle, within 250 miles of the front line," adding that "from high altitudes, target identification makes visual day bombing difficult. For accurate bombing therefore, there is a continuing need both by day and by night to be able to mark targets accurately. There will therefore be a requirement for an aircraft to mark visually for a medium-range Canberra force."

However, the continuing development of a suitable radar system was slow, and with the radar-equipped V-Force on the horizon, the target marker Canberra eventually seemed like an expensive luxury. The Canberra B.Mk.5 was therefore dropped and English Electric opted to use the prototype as the basis of what would become the B.Mk.8 intruder variant. For this new Canberra, English Electric's designers decided to revise the crew compartment layout that had been employed since the beginning of Canberra production. The forward fuselage behind the cockpit would be removed and a new fighter-type cockpit and canopy installed, offset to port with a standard windscreen and a slimmer perspex

canopy combined with a conventional windscreen. The original circular 'glasshouse' canopy had been a controversial choice from the start. It provided the Canberra pilot with good all-round visibility but it wasn't optically perfect, and a small circular porthole named Direct Vision (DV) had to be incorporated into the canopy so that the pilot had at least some good clear forward vision through the flat panel (the T.Mk.4 employed two flat panels, to cater for the side-by-side seating) and a means of allowing outside air into the cockpit if necessary. Peering through the porthole was not the most elegant of procedures, but the big bubble canopy was normally adequate for the Canberra's high level bombing role.

Not so suitable was the canopy's ability to gather and capture heat, which often made conditions for the crew intolerable when the aircraft was on the ground in direct sunlight. It was obvious to everyone that a new intruder Canberra needed the new fighter-type cockpit arrangement and it was also proposed that the navigator/bomb-aimer's seat should be moved forward and repositioned beside the pilot, inside the fuselage. This was a logical arrangement, but only the pilot was to be given an ejection seat and it was decided that the navigator would rely instead on manual egress through the fuselage door. This was undoubtedly a bad decision for an aircraft that was destined ▶

Converting the Mk.5 Canberra into the Mk.8 interdictor took just six months. Its first flight was made from Samlesbury on 23 July 1954, in the hands of Roland Beamont. Two months later the aircraft appeared at the SBAC Farnborough show, from where it is pictured, high over Hampshire. *(Photo: Aeroplane)*

◄▲ B(I).Mk.8 flight testing, including aerodynamic investigation of the new fighter-style cockpit canopy, was conducted from Warton. The aircraft was flown with the canopy removed and with various stores attached to its wing pylons. Further trials were devoted to the ventral gun pack in the bomb bay. The new canopy and windscreen were immediately recognised as far superior to the original blown canopy and ideally suited to the low-level strike and interdictor role. *(Photos: Aeroplane)*

➤ WT340 was the second Mk.8 Canberra produced by Shorts. Assigned to No.88 Squadron in Germany, it is seen in "clean" configuration without wingtip fuel tanks, although for most operations the Mk.8 routinely carried these. The tanks could be jettisoned in flight when empty, although this was never done during peacetime training. Also visible is the aircraft's 'Homing Eye' tail warning radar, housed in the tailcone. *(Photo: Aeroplane)*

to spend most of its flying time at low level and even more than 70 years later it is difficult to understand why the 'intruder' Canberra's peculiar arrangement was adopted, especially when the aircraft had already captured the interest of the USAF and the American manufacturer Martin had swiftly devised a much better tandem seating arrangement for it's B-57 derivative. Why English Electric never embraced a similar design (or simply adopted the design created by Martin) is a mystery.

Rather more logical was the decision to design a gun pack for the aircraft, comprising four Hispano 20mm cannon with 520 rounds per gun, all contained in a fairing that could be attached to the lower fuselage of the Canberra, leaving the forward portion of the bomb bay to be used for other ordnance. Additionally, under wing hard points would also be installed so that a 1,000lb free fall bomb could be carried or a Matra rocket launcher, plus other weapons. Most importantly, there would be a provision to carry a tactical nuclear bomb internally.

Over a six month period VX185 was rebuilt and it emerged for its first flight as the prototype B(I).Mk.8 on 23 July 1954. A production contract followed which also included a batch of conversions, intended to supplement the main force of new Mk.8 aircraft. The conversions were applied to 19 B.Mk.6 aircraft (plus three more that were subsequently ordered) that were modified to carry the new Boulton Paul gun pack with the necessary weapons bay strengthening and alterations, plus the new wing pylon provisions. However, the forward fuselage complete with the original 'greenhouse' canopy remained unchanged, and as such these aircraft were designated as the Canberra B(I).Mk.6 (the 'I' denoting the interdictor role). These new Canberras were soon deployed to Germany where their relatively modest range was less of an issue. Just minutes from the East German border, they were well placed to be called into action, but it wasn't only the Canberra's range that dictated the shift to Germany. It was the lack of available space on the UK mainland where the RAF was simply running

This view of the Canberra B(I).Mk.8 illustrates the revised forward fuselage, with the offset pilot's canopy and the modified nose glazing with additional side windows. Also of note are the demarcation lines on the wing leading edges, these being common to Mk.6 and Mk.8 derivatives with internal fuel tanks. *(Photo: Aeroplane)*

out of airfields that could accommodate the ever-expanding bomber force. Moving to Germany made sense as suitable airfields were already available, and the bomber force would immediately be much closer to its projected area of operations.

NATO thinking at the time assumed that any confrontation with the Soviet Union would begin with a huge influx of conventional forces from the East, with countless armoured columns progressing across Germany's northern plains. With a perceived numerical inferiority, the West's conventional forces couldn't hope to contain this kind of attack for more than a few days and although the RAF's Canberra intruders would clearly be called on to support NATO forces through the delivery of conventional bombs and the provision of heavy cannon fire, it was almost inevitable that they would be called on to deliver tactical nuclear bombs if the advance was not stopped.

Likewise, Britain had adopted a policy of a strategic deterrence and the Canberras would, if needed, act as part of this retaliatory strike capability. The provision of a nuclear capability for RAF Germany's Canberras was made possible through the introduction of an agreement ('Project E') between the British and US governments made in 1957 to enable American nuclear weapons to be carried by RAF aircraft. Britain's ability to produce atomic weapons in large numbers was a great challenge (because of a woeful lack of resources and money) and as the perceived Soviet threat became greater and more serious, it was accepted that the US and UK would have to co-operate if the West was to have any hope of presenting the USSR with a credible nuclear deterrent. Part of the Project E agreement stated that if a full-scale war should break out, it would probably consist of two phases, one being of comparatively

Manufactured in 1968, XM244 was delivered to No.16 Squadron. It was also operated by No.3 Squadron but returned to the former unit and (like many of the unit's Canberras) received a striking red/white "sharkmouth" marking on its nose, together with a yellow/black band around the fuselage and the unit's saint emblem on the tail fin. *(Photo: Tim McLelland collection)*

A No.14 Squadron Canberra B(I).Mk.8 inside an operational readiness shelter. Canberras armed with a single Mk.7 Thor atomic bomb (provided by the US) were held on 24-hour quick reaction alert. The weapon had a yield of up to 60 kilotons – three times that of the atomic bomb dropped on Hiroshima. *(Photo: Tim McLelland collection)*

XM276 spent some time operating with the RAE and Marshalls on trials work before being assigned to RAF Germany. It joined No.3 Squadron in 1966 and remained with that unit until 1971 when it was withdrawn and returned to BAC. It was then refurbished and sold to Peru, where it became aircraft No.256, delivered in 1978. *(Photo: Tim McLelland collection)*

The Canberra B(I).Mk.8's offset cockpit and canopy are evident in this view. Otherwise similar to the Canberra Mk.6 in terms of structure and systems, and forward fuselage and nose section shape and dimensions, its cockpit arrangement gave the Mk.8 a strikingly different appearance. *(Photo: Aeroplane)*

➤ Completed in August 1958, XM245 was not delivered to the RAF. Instead, it was assigned to Boulton Paul at Seighford, where it was used for trials of the Blue Silk Doppler radar navigation system. It remained there until 1963 when it was returned to the manufacturer for refurbishment. It then returned to test flying (primarily with Marshalls) before finally reaching the RAF in March 1966. It served with No.3 Squadron until June 1972 and eventually found its way to the Nordhorn weapons range where it was used as a ground target.
(Photo: FAST Museum)

short duration 'characterised by an intensive exchange of atomic blows' and a secondary phase of reduced intensity. Throughout these exchanges, survivability would be a key concern and this implied that the Allied response should be 'conducted with maximum possible speed and effectiveness, and with its weight of effort unwaveringly exerted against the highest priority targets.' This meant that the RAF and USAF would have to operate together with fully co-ordinated strike plans that ensured the best use of resources and avoided 'overlap' wherever possible. It was also stated that the Allied counter air offensive would require 'heavy co-ordinated attacks against airfields, logistic facilities, control centres and command headquarters' and this task would rely heavily upon the RAF's Canberras. Plans were made to equip the

Canberra with a British-designed tactical atomic bomb (Red Beard) but with development and quantity production taking a great deal of time (and the knowledge that Red Beard was a less-than-reliable weapon), the Project E agreement enabled the Canberra to be nuclear-capable within a much shorter time scale, with only relatively small modifications to the aircraft being necessary to enable the Mk.7 'Thor' weapon to be carried. The Mk.7 bomb was 15ft long and weighed only 1,650lb. The Canberra could carry it comfortably but the bomb bay doors needed to be altered in order to accommodate it, and baffle plates had to be fitted so that the bomb bay doors could be safely opened at the higher speeds necessary for release of the American weapon. The bomb was fitted with a radar altimeter that enabled the weapon to be

detonated at around 1,500ft above the selected target (an 'air burst'), ensuring that the maximum destructive effect was achieved. With Uranium 235 fissionable elements located in the warhead, the amount of material inserted into the warhead core could be varied so that different yields could be selected anywhere from 8 kilotons through to 61 kilotons (three times the power of the bomb dropped on Hiroshima). Precisely why the yield might be varied is open to question as there would obviously have been little value in restricting the bomb's destructive power (the higher yields were expected to be used against large targets such as airfields) and it seems likely that had the bomb ever been used in a real wartime situation, they would all have been released at their highest yield setting.

A pair of Canberra B(I).Mk.8s from No.16 Squadron outside their hangar at Laarbruch. As with many RAF Canberra units, the squadron's ground crews have devised a portable sunshade to keep direct sunlight off the canopy and cockpit. Excessive cockpit heat was a problem that affected all Canberra variants.
(Photo: Aeroplane)

WT363 was completed at Samlesbury in January 1957. It was delivered to No.14 squadron and subsequently transferred to No.59 Squadron, as illustrated. On 11 June 1968 it collided with XM278 whilst flying a low level mission over Germany, and crashed near Roermond. *(Photo: Tim McLelland collection)*

Pictured during a sortie from its base in Germany while serving with No.3 Squadron, WT362 overflies Stonehenge. This aircraft was also operated by No.88 Squadron and remained active until 1972. The main sections of the airframe were destroyed on the fire dump at Catterick although the nose section was saved for preservation. *(Photo: Tim McLelland collection)*

This trio of Canberras was assigned to the Royal Radar Establishment, based at Defford. The two closest to the camera have Mk.8 forward fuselages but were in fact B.Mk.2s. VN828 was the second prototype Canberra and received a Mk.8 nose section during its use as a trials aircraft. It made its last flight in 1961. WJ646 was similarly equipped and subsequently moved to Boscombe Down by road for fire fighting use.
(Photo: Tim McLelland collection)

WT345 displays the unusual unit markings of No.59 Squadron, comprising a red and white triangle and a black exclamation mark. The aircraft also operated with Nos.3, 14 and 16 Squadrons before being retired in 1971. It was then used as an airfield decoy at Laarbruch before being broken up. *(Photo: Tim McLelland collection)*

The use of the Mk.7 bomb was undoubtedly an ideal arrangement for the RAF, USAF and NATO. However there were difficulties to overcome, not least the ways in which America retained control of the weapons. The Canberras were assigned to QRA (Quick Reaction Alert) duties and a number of aircraft were kept at constant readiness for immediate launch, should a conflict break out at short notice. The QRA Canberras were housed in their own alert hangars, surrounded by high security fencing and kept under armed guard.

RAF crews were rotated through QRA duty for 24-hour periods on alternate days for a period of two weeks at a time. At least one USAF officer was always present inside the QRA compound so that he could give final authorisation for use of the weapon if ever required. Practice scrambles were often performed although they were usually terminated before reaching engine start. Routine flying training was performed but nuclear stores were obviously not carried and small inert training rounds were usually used, and dropped on weapons ranges either in Germany (Nordhorn) or occasionally in the UK.

The LABS (Low Altitude Bombing System) was employed as the means of delivering the Mk.7 bomb to its target, requiring the Canberra to perform some surprisingly dynamic manoeuvres. From a height of 250ft and at a speed of 434kt, the Canberra would be pulled up into a 3.4g climb and the Mk.7 bomb would be released automatically at a pre-determined angle (usually around 60º). However, if the target was difficult to locate, this meant that no suitable IP (Initial Point) could be used (the IP being a clearly visible geographical point on the track towards the target) and so the Canberra pilot would be obliged to fly directly over the target and release the bomb at an angle of approximately 110 degrees (sometimes referred to as an 'over the shoulder' release). With both types of manoeuvre the Canberra would eventually be inverted in a descent at approximately 5,500ft, and at this stage the pilot applied rudder and aileron to turn the aircraft around into an erect descent. If the

Following its completion at Samlesbury in October 1956, XH209 was retained by English Electric for the installation of low-level bombing system equipment. It was then used by Marshalls and the RAE before being allocated to RAF Germany, where it joined No.59 Squadron and then No.16 Squadron, as here. Withdrawn in 1972, the aircraft became an airfield decoy at Gütersloh. *(Photo: Godfrey Mangion)*

manoeuvre was executed too soon the aircraft would be in imminent danger of stalling (speed would be down to around 160 kt) but if the manoeuvre was left too late the aircraft would be in a very steep inverted dive from which recovery might be impossible. Consequently, practising LABS deliveries was an important and regular part of RAFG operations. The same techniques were also introduced for UK Canberra squadrons although they remained associated only with conventional HE weapons. The RAFG Canberras, by comparison, were almost exclusively dedicated to the nuclear role, but as part of a NATO agreement, each Canberra squadron was permitted to stand down from its assignment to SACEUR (Supreme Allied Commander Europe) for short periods every year, usually for one month.

During this period the crews had an opportunity to operate the Canberras in the purely national interdictor role for which the Canberra Mk.8 had been designed, and Armament Practice Camps were set up for this purpose, normally at RAF Luqa, Malta with live bomb deliveries and gun firing taking place on ranges in Libya. However,

the Canberra was also eventually assigned a nuclear role much further afield, following the formation of the Central Treaty Organization (also known as the Baghdad Pact) in 1955. As part of this agreement, two Canberra squadrons (Nos 32 and 73) were deployed to Akrotiri, Cyprus during 1957 with two more units (Nos. 6 and 249 Squadrons) following a few weeks later from Coningsby. By this stage the Canberra had also deployed to the Far East, Nos 9, 12, 101, and 617 Squadrons having provided detachments in support of Operation Firedog (the Malayan Emergency) from 1955 onwards. No.45 Squadron based at Tengah in Singapore, began re-equipping with Canberras late in 1957. Unfortunately,

Manufactured during 1955, Canberra B(I).MK.6 WT341 served with Nos 3, 14, 16 (as shown) and 88 Squadrons before being withdrawn in 1972. It was then used by Little Rissington's fire section as a training airframe. *(Photo: Aeroplane)*

After being operated by No.16 Squadron, XM267 was allocated to No.3 Squadron. It remained with the unit until December 1970, when it crashed on approach to RAF Akrotiri. *(Photo: Godfrey Mangion)*

Wearing the markings of No.14 Squadron, XK951 is on approach to RAF Luqa shortly before its transfer to No.16 Squadron. It served out its RAF career with No.3 Squadron before being withdrawn in 1972. It was then returned to BAC for refurbishment and sold to Peru as aircraft No.248, arriving in country during April 1975.

(Photo: Godfrey Mangion)

On the runway at RAF Luqa, Canberra B(I).Mk.8 WT336 wears the markings of No.14 Squadron. It has standard Dark Sea Grey and Dark Green camouflage over Light Aircraft Grey undersides, and silver tip tanks. The port engine appears to have a faded cowling panel taken from another aircraft.

(Photo: Godfrey Mangion)

WV787 was the 90th production B.Mk.2. Initially delivered to Armstrong Siddeley Motors at Bitteswell for Sapphire engine development, it was subsequently transferred to Boulton Paul at Seighford, where it was modified to carry radar equipment under test for the Blackburn NA.39 (Buccaneer). Refitted with a Mk.8 forward fuselage and Buccaneer radome, it later became the aerodynamic test vehicle for the Canberra T.Mk.22. In later years the aircraft went to Boscombe Down, where it was used as a sprayer on behalf of the Chemical Defence Establishment at Porton Down. Finally, WV787 was used as a sprayer in icing trials for various programmes, including Concorde. The aircraft was retired in 1983 and went to Abingdon's Battle Damage Repair Flight, before being rescued by the Newark Air Museum, with which it remained on display in 2024.

(Photos: Tim McLelland collection & Michael Freer)

Canberra B.Mk.2 WJ643 was delivered directly to Ferranti at Turnhouse, where it was used on air interception (AI) radar trials, refitted with a Mk.8 forward fuselage. It remained with Ferranti and the RAE for many years, operating from Turnhouse and West Freugh. Later, WJ643 was assigned to laser rangefinder testing in support of the Jaguar programme and eventually moved to RAE Farnborough, where it was repainted in RAE colours. The aircraft supported various research programmes (including forward-looking infra-red development) and was repainted in the RAE's 'Raspberry Ripple' paint scheme shortly before its retirement in 1981 and transfer to Shoeburyness, where parts of the airframe might conceivably survive.
(Photos: Tim McLelland collection & FAST Museum)

the Canberra was far from suited to the operational requirements and conditions that were assigned to it in the Far East, as the official records of the Malayan campaign indicate: "The Canberra carried half the bomb load of Lincolns and their cruising speed of 250 knots at the optimum bombing height required more elaborate navigational aids and made map reading impracticable and visual bomb aiming difficult. The pilot had a poorer visibility than in a Lincoln and the Canberra could not be flown at night or in close formation and could not be employed in a strafing role. They suffered, in common with all jet aircraft in the tropics, from a serious limitation in their endurance at low level, which precluded the possibility of postponing or delaying an air strike once they were airborne. This was a serious disadvantage in the uncertain weather conditions of Malaya, especially in 1958 when Canberras were operating in the northern part of the country, far from their parent base at Tengah, and this was reflected in an increase

in the rate of abortive air strikes when they replaced Lincolns. When flown at their normal speed at low altitude the swirl vanes of Canberra engines suffered badly from metal fatigue in the hot, turbulent air, which also made flying conditions difficult for their pilots. For those Canberras that were not fitted with Godfrey air coolers, sun canopies, cooling trollies and external compressed air supplies had to be employed to combat the danger of loss of body weight through sweating which could amount to as much as 3lb per sortie. Both from the point of view of maintenance and flying conditions Lincolns were preferable to Canberras in the type of campaign that prevailed in Malaya."

It was somewhat ironic that in this instance the Canberra was found to be inferior to the aircraft that it had been designed to replace, but this odd situation only applied to Malaya. In contrast, the Canberra was ideally suited to other areas of operation, especially the European theatre. Eventually, the Akrotiri Canberra squadrons were re-equipped with Canberra B.Mk.15

and B.Mk.16 aircraft, these being 'tropicalised' derivatives of the B.6 variant. With these, the Akrotiri Strike Wing was able to embrace a nuclear capability and Red Beard weapons were assigned to Cyprus for this role. The wing remained active as a strike/attack force until 1969 when the Canberras were withdrawn and replaced by Vulcans drawn from the Coningsby and Cottesmore wings. Of course, most of the RAF's Canberra bomber force was eventually replaced by the new Vulcan which enjoyed much better range, altitude and bomb-carrying capability, and as the V-Force (Valiants, Vulcans, and Victors) came into service, the Canberra was gradually withdrawn from its pure bomber role. However, operations in Germany with the nuclear-capable interdictor force continued into the 1970s and it wasn't until until the Buccaneer was introduced into service that the RAF finally withdrew the last of its Canberras from the offensive role for which the type had been designed a quarter of a century previously. ❖

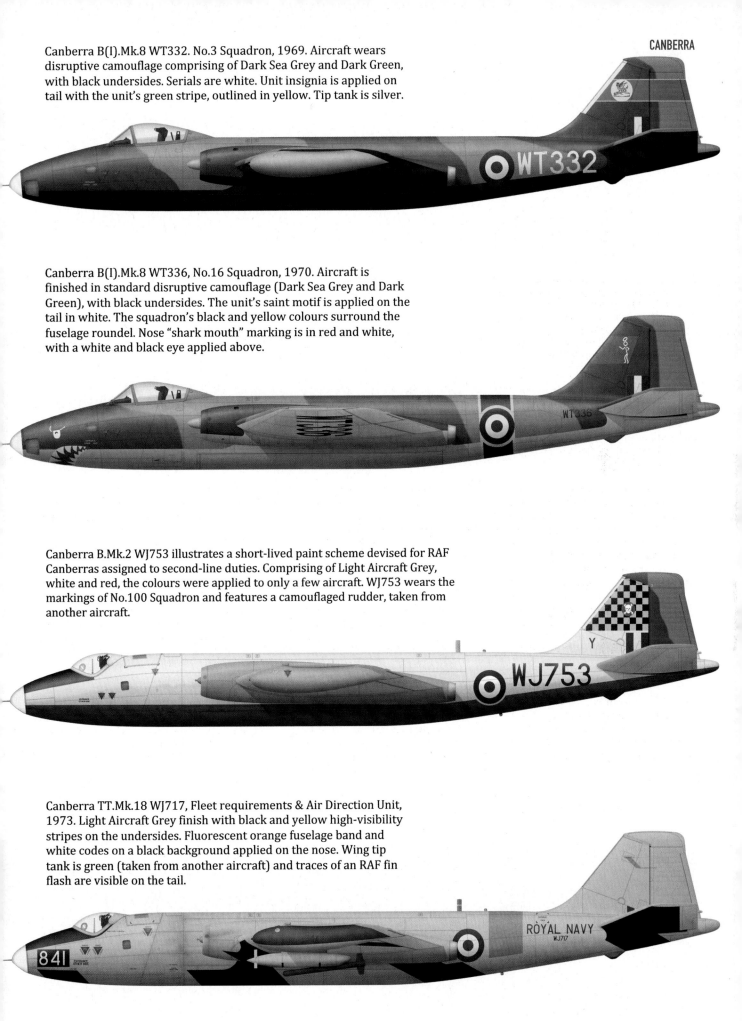

Canberra B(I).Mk.8 WT332. No.3 Squadron, 1969. Aircraft wears disruptive camouflage comprising of Dark Sea Grey and Dark Green, with black undersides. Serials are white. Unit insignia is applied on tail with the unit's green stripe, outlined in yellow. Tip tank is silver.

Canberra B(I).Mk.8 WT336, No.16 Squadron, 1970. Aircraft is finished in standard disruptive camouflage (Dark Sea Grey and Dark Green), with black undersides. The unit's saint motif is applied on the tail in white. The squadron's black and yellow colours surround the fuselage roundel. Nose "shark mouth" marking is in red and white, with a white and black eye applied above.

Canberra B.Mk.2 WJ753 illustrates a short-lived paint scheme devised for RAF Canberras assigned to second-line duties. Comprising of Light Aircraft Grey, white and red, the colours were applied to only a few aircraft. WJ753 wears the markings of No.100 Squadron and features a camouflaged rudder, taken from another aircraft.

Canberra TT.Mk.18 WJ717, Fleet requirements & Air Direction Unit, 1973. Light Aircraft Grey finish with black and yellow high-visibility stripes on the undersides. Fluorescent orange fuselage band and white codes on a black background applied on the nose. Wing tip tank is green (taken from another aircraft) and traces of an RAF fin flash are visible on the tail.

Drawings by Chris Sandham-Bailey (www.inkworm.co.uk)

The last Canberras in RAF service were a handful of PR.Mk.9s with No.39 (1 PRU) Squadron at Marham. This view shows the Mk.9's offset fighter-type canopy, larger engine nacelles and fin-mounted radar warning receiver.
(Photo: Tim McLelland)

BEYOND THE BOMBER

Designed as a jet bomber, the Canberra's versatility enabled the aircraft to perform a wide range of specialised roles

Canberra PR.Mk.9 XH175 over the Mediterranean whilst serving with NO.39 Squadron, based at Luqa, Malta.

XH170 illustrates the Canberra PR.Mk.9's modified wing structure, with extended chord inboard of the engines, and extended wing tips. The MK.9 fleet was initially painted overall High Speed Silver but after only a few years this was replaced with tactical grey/green camouflage. Full colour national insignia lasted until the early 1970s when 'toned-down' red/blue insignia was applied. *(Photo: Tim McLelland collection & Godfrey Mangion)*

The diminishing need for Canberra bombers might have spelled the end for a less versatile aircraft but the Canberra remained in RAF service through the 1960s and 1970s and went on to perform a wide variety of tasks, many of which were very different to the bomber role for which it had been designed. Most notably, the basic bomber design was developed for photographic reconnaissance operations, beginning with the PR.Mk.3 prototype (VX181) that completed its maiden flight on 19 March 1950, long before the Canberra was retired from the bombing role. Developed in response to Specification PR.31/56, the aircraft was essentially a B.Mk.2 airframe with a 14in fuselage extension ahead of the wing leading edge. This additional space housed six F52 oblique cameras, although a single F49 vertical survey camera was also normally installed too, and alternative equipment fits could be installed as required, including two F89 cameras for night photography. Additional

fuel capacity was also provided, and the bomb bay was modified to carry 1.75in flares in a specially designed crate, for night photography. Introducing the PR.Mk.3 into service was far from smooth, thanks to the recurrence of airframe vibrations that had originally manifested themselves when the prototype Canberra first flew. Modifications to the aircraft (particularly behind the cockpit) reduced the vibrations to an acceptable level, but the PR.Mk.3's longer fuselage caused the problem to return. English Electric anticipated this, and opted to simply impose a Mach 0.75 speed limitation on the aircraft, as opposed to the 0.84 limit that was applied to the B.Mk.2 fleet. But when the aircraft was evaluated at Boscombe Down, the RAF's test pilots were not satisfied with it and English Electric was obliged to rectify the problem rather than avoid it. Wisely, the company's technicians decided to eradicate the problem from the Canberra design as a whole and the elevators (particularly the mass balances)

were modified, while large strengthening plates were fitted to the fuselage sides, and these became standard on all Canberras that were subsequently manufactured. The PR.Mk.3 entered RAF service late in 1952 and was quickly introduced into both UK and Germany-based squadrons.

The Canberra B.Mk.6, fitted with Avon Mk.109 engines (each rated at 7,500lb) and additional fuel tanks in the wing leading edges, was also modified for photographic reconnaissance use, resulting in the PR.Mk.7. Featuring the same camera installation and airframe modifications as applied to the B.Mk.2 to create the PR.Mk.3, the first PR.Mk.7 made its maiden flight on 16 August 1953. It was introduced into RAF service swiftly and smoothly and gradually replaced the 'shorter legged' PR.Mk.3 both in the UK and overseas. Perhaps most notably, the Canberra PR.Mk.7 was employed on clandestine reconnaissance missions along the peripheries of the Warsaw Pact states, providing vital imagery of Soviet defences ➤

ALL THIS PAGE: No.39 Squadron was a long-term operator of the Canberra PR.Mk.9, based at RAF Luqa, Malta and latterly in the UK, at Wyton and Marham. Many of the unit's aircraft operated from Luqa with wing tip fuel tanks attached for longer-ranged sorties from the Mediterranean base. The tanks were attached to the original B.Mk.2 hardpoints, inboard of the Mk.9's extended tips. (Photos: Tim McLelland collection & Godfrey Mangion)

and military installations, all of which was of immeasurable use to the US and UK governments.

These Cold War missions also enabled Strategic Air Command and Bomber Command to pinpoint targets for the growing fleets of SAC B-47 and B-52 bombers, and the RAF's Valiants, Vulcans and Victors. Operating at heights of 50,000ft or more, the Canberra PR.Mk.7 was ideally suited to such long-range missions, although it gradually became obvious that Soviet Surface to Air Missiles (SAM) would soon be capable of intercepting reconnaissance aircraft at such altitudes. If the Canberra was to remain useful as a viable reconnaissance platform it would have to fly much higher, at altitudes of 65,000ft or more. English Electric's designers

concluded that by installing a more powerful engine (the 11,250lb Avon RA.24 that was being developed for the Lightning) and increasing the Canberra's wingspan, a new high-altitude derivative could be produced. This resulted in the HA PR.Mk.9 (HA denoting the aircraft's specialised high altitude capability). Extending the Canberra's wingspan was not a simple process, as the resulting changes affected the aircraft's high-speed trim conditions and caused buffet problems. The solution was to increase the wing's area inboard of the engine fairings, extending the chord quite considerably. A factory-fresh Canberra PR. Mk.7 (WH793) was allocated to the project and modified by Napier to evaluate the redesigned wing and more powerful engines. The modified aircraft (essentially a

re-winged PR.Mk.7) made its first flight on 8 July 1955 from Cranfield.

Unfortunately, the aircraft didn't achieve the altitude performance that English Electric had hoped for, as the larger wing created a significant amount of induced drag when the aircraft was at high angles of attack at high altitude. This negated the additional thrust provided by the new engines, and a maximum altitude of 60,000ft was the best that the aircraft could achieve. This was still a great improvement over the PR.Mk.7, and with two very powerful engines installed, the PR.Mk.9 was endowed with a rate of climb that outclassed many contemporary fighter aircraft. It was enough to convince the Air Staff that the aircraft should be produced for the RAF and the first production

These photographs illustrate the stark difference in colour schemes applied to the Canberra PR.Mk.9 from initial service entry, when the aircraft were finished in high-speed silver, beyond 2000, when hemp and low-visibility markings were worn. Externally, the PR.Mk.9 changed very little over decades of operational use, the only significant difference being the addition of radar warning receivers at the fin leading edge and tail cone.
(Photos: Aeroplane & RAF Marham)

Through the latter years of the Canberra PR.Mk.9's operational life, the dwindling fleet of aircraft were painted in a hemp camouflage scheme, primarily designed to provide a degree of camouflage for the aircraft whilst on the ground. During operations in Afghanistan, a small number of aircraft were repainted in a (removable) light grey livery, deemed to be more suitable for that theatre.
(Photos: Crown Copyright & Tim McLelland collection)

◄ The partially open hinged nose cone reveals the cramped cockpit occupied by the PR.Mk.9's navigator, including instrument panel and periscope. Also visible is one of the two tiny windows that provided the only source of daylight and outside vision for the navigator.
(Photo: Tim McLelland collection)

example (WH129) was built by Shorts. It made its first flight on 27 July 1958.

In addition to powerful engines and larger wings, the production-standard PR.Mk.9 also featured a completely re-designed forward fuselage with a fighter-style cockpit and canopy similar to the design that had been applied to the Canberra B.Mk.8. However, for the PR.Mk.9 the cockpit canopy was designed to hinge open, enabling the pilot to access the cockpit by means of an external ladder. The navigator was housed in a new position, forward of the pilot in a centrally positioned ejection seat in the aircraft's nose, accessed by a hinged nose cone. It was a much more satisfactory arrangement for the pilot, but the navigator's position was arguably less than ideal. With only a tiny window to the left and right of the upper nose, the navigator's compartment was almost light-free (ideal for reconnaissance work), but it was also incredibly cramped and claustrophobic. On the other hand, the navigator did finally get an ejection seat.

The Canberra PR.Mk.9's development suffered a major blow on 11 October 1958 when WH129 crashed in Liverpool Bay,

killing the navigator. The aircraft's inner wing root skin attachment had failed when it was subjected to a 5g turn, allowing the wing skin to peel backwards under the heavy aerodynamic load, thereby causing the wing structure to fail. The wing attachments were redesigned to enable the aircraft to withstand greater loads and tested on XH136, which successfully performed a 5.1g turn at full power without any problems. With this modification accepted, the RAF's operational Canberra PR.Mk.9s possessed not only an adequate altitude performance, but also enjoyed a remarkable rate of climb, outstanding manoeuvrability, and a built-in strength that enabled the aircraft to be handled like a fighter whenever necessary.

Unlike the earlier Mk.3 and Mk.7, the more versatile PR.Mk.9 was progressively modified throughout its service life to accommodate new cameras and sensors as they emerged, providing the RAF with an outstanding reconnaissance platform that continued to perform well for much longer than either the RAF or English Electric could have imagined. Among many other new sensors (including infra-red line scan systems), a fixed-focus 36in mirror lens

Outwardly similar to a regular PR.Mk.9, XH132 was the sole Canberra SC.Mk.1, manufactured by Shorts as a trials and research aircraft. Primarily used for airborne intercept radar testing, it also flew a wide variety of other trials during its long service life. Originally finished in a dazzling, albeit short-lived overall fluorescent orange scheme (as here), it later flew in both silver and white before becoming a familiar sight in RAE 'Raspberry Ripple'. *(Photos: Aeroplane)*

Canberra PR.Mk.7 WH793 after being re-fitted with enlarged wings and more powerful engines during PR.Mk.9 development.
(Photo: Aeroplane)

PR.Mk.7 WH793 trialled the PR.Mk.9 powerplant and wing layout. The modified wing structure included much larger inner wing chord trailling edge extensions than those adopted for production PR.Mk.9s. Its developmental work complete, WH793 was assigned to the RAE for high-altitude atmospheric research, with sensors attached to a long nose boom replacing its original nose. BAC borrowed it from February 1973 as a Concorde chase aircraft, based at Fairford. When this task ended in 1975, WH793 was stored at Farnborough before being removed to Bedford for disposal.
(Photos: Aeroplane & Adrian Balch collection)

camera was introduced, capable of producing astonishingly detailed images of ground objects from heights of between 49,000ft and 51,000ft. Although the RAF was understandably reluctant to demonstrate just how capable the Canberra PR.Mk.9's systems really were, published photographs of the clock face of Big Ben's tower taken from over the Isle of Wight certainly demonstrated the potential of its cameras.

These Canberras provided valuable reconnaissance data during both the Bosnia and Afghanistan operations, enabling Allied forces to obtain imagery when it was needed, instead of being obliged to wait for a reconnaissance satellite to make a suitable orbit. It is also likely that Canberras supported British forces during the Falklands conflict, operating from bases in Chile, although for political reasons this matter was never publicised. However, the fact that three former RAF Canberra PR.Mk.9s were

supplied to Chile after the war suggests that there may well have been some sort of 'repayment in kind' for Chile's support. Such was the Canberra's usefulness to the RAF (and other government agencies) that it remained in service until 2006, employing a camera system derived from the Senior Year Electro-Optical Relay System (SYERS) installation used on the US Air Force U-2S. No.39 (1 PRU) Squadron disbanded in July, marked by a flypast completing what was the very last operational RAF Canberra sortie. Official retirement of the type by the RAF occurred on the morning of 31 July when XH131 arrived at Kemble and was handed over to a civilian buyer. This marked the very end of the RAF's association with the Canberra, which had begun on 25 May 1951 when the aircraft entered service at Binbrook.

The Canberra's simple and reliable design enabled the aircraft to be used for a wide

variety of tasks, and with so many redundant airframes being available, it was perhaps unsurprising that it was assigned to many second-line roles with the RAF, Royal Navy and other government agencies. Following production of the reconnaissance Canberra PR.Mk.9, the next Canberra derivative to emerge was the U.Mk.10, a specialised pilotless target drone, primarily designed to support missile tests that were being conducted at the Woomera range in Australia. Short Brothers was contracted to produce a batch of conversions (from B.Mk.2 airframes) and the first was ferried to Woomera in 1959. With 'near miss' telemetry on board, the aircraft were normally used for tests involving missiles with inert warheads, as live tests could have meant the destruction of the aircraft.

The Canberra U.Mk.10 remained in use through the 1960s and a similar variant (the U.Mk.14) was developed for various naval missile trials conducted in Malta during the early 1960s. The Canberra T.Mk.11 was designed in response to a requirement for a radar trainer to support the RAF's Javelin fighter squadrons. Equipped with the Javelin's radar system (housed in a bulky nose cone, fixed to the forward nose attachment joint), the T.Mk.11 enabled students to practice the art of airborne interception and a batch of eight B.Mk.2 airframes was converted for the role by Boulton Paul. They joined No.228 OCU at Leeming in 1959, remaining in service until 1961. The redundant airframes were then transferred to West Raynham where they were assigned to

A magnificent formation of Canberra T.Mk.17As from
No. 360 Squadron shortly before their retirement.
(Photo: Gordon Bain)

◄ The T.Mk.17 was undoubtedly the ugliest of all the specialised Canberra versions that were produced. Electronic jammers and sensors sprouted from the aircraft's nose and tail, with additional aerials appearing on the fuselage and wings. However, the T.Mk.17 and T.Mk.17A were immensely useful to the British armed forces, providing a simulated electronic threat during countless training exercises. Initially, two Canberra T.Mk.17 units were formed, with No.360 Squadron becoming the long-established operator of the type. Unusually, the squadron was a joint RAF and Royal Navy unit. *(Photo: Aeroplane)*

WD955 was for many years the oldest Canberra in service, having been delivered to the RAF in December 1951 as a Canberra B.Mk.2. In recognition of this distinction, it received a red tail, complete with No.360 Squadron's lightning flash emblem. Towards the end of the T.Mk.17's service, they were painted in a hemp and light aircraft grey livery, with red and blue national insignia. A few aircraft (as illustrated) subsequently received low visibility pink and paul blue insignia.
(Photo: Gordon Bain)

◄ Canberra WH664 was manufactured in 1952 as a B.Mk.2. It was operated by the RAE's 'Swifter' Flight before being returned to BAC for modification to T. Mk.17 standard. Serving with Nos. 360 and 361 Squadrons at Watton, it later moved to Cottesmore and finally to Wyton, where it was withdrawn in 1991. It was eventually scrapped on site. *(Photo: Michael Freer)*

This colourful quartet of Canberras was at Luqa in the early 1970s. The aircraft with yellow and black undersides is TT.Mk.18 WJ682 from No.7 Squadron. In the foreground is the nose of a T.Mk.4 trainer, while in the distance are two B.Mk.2s from No.100 Squadron. One carries the short-lived red, white and grey scheme applied to a few Canberras during this period. (Photo: Godfrey Mangion)

Canberra B.Mk.2 WH718 (above and below) was converted into TT.Mk.18 target tug configuration in 1968. Used for pre-service trials at Warton, Boscombe Down and Tarrant Rushton, the aircraft then entered service with No.7 Squadron at St.Mawgan before eventually moving to Wyton to join No.100 Squadron. (Photos: Tim McLelland collection)

◄ This rare picture shows a Canberra TT.Mk.18 from No.7 Squadron trailing a live Rushton target. For normal training sorties the target was trailed from its launcher pod at considerable distance, with flares being ignited to aid visual tracking. Recording sensors in the target enabled 'miss distances' to be established. (Photo: Tim McLelland) ➤

The Canberra TT.Mk.18 was also employed by the Royal Navy, the Fleet Requirements and Air Direction Unit (FRADU) at Yeovilton operating a fleet of these target tugs in support of Royal Navy training. Many former RAF machines were also eventually transferred to the unit. Various types of target were trailed from the wing-mounted Rushton winches, including missile simulators and banners. In addition, the aircraft was used as a 'silent' target, acting as a threat simulator for radar tracking. WJ614 was operated by Nos. 7, 85, and 100 Squadrons before joining FRADU in 1972. *(Photos: Tim McLelland collection)*

Canberra TT.Mk.18s in formation for a publicity photograph shortly before FRADU withdrew the type. They are devoid of tip tanks and targets in a rarely seen configuration usually reserved for 'silent' missions in which towed targets were unnecessary. *(Photo: Crown Copyright)*

▲ Canberra T.Mk.19 WH724 from No.100 Squadron, at Leuchars in 1972. It was withdrawn from use in 1976 and dumped at Shawbury, where it was eventually dismantled. *(Photo: Tim McLelland collection)*

◄ The Canberra T.Mk.11 was a conversion of the standard B.Mk.2 airframe with AI radar installed in a nose radome. Used to train Javelin fighter crews, the T.Mk.11s had been withdrawn by the late 1960s, after which they were refurbished, their radar equipment removed and ballast installed. Redesignated T.Mk.19, they flew as continuation trainers and 'silent' targets with Nos. 85, 100, and 7 Squadrons. *(Photo: Tim McLelland collection)*

target facilities duties, flying sorties in support of the RAF's Lightning interceptor squadrons and (occasionally) Bloodhound SAM units. From 1965 the T.Mk.11s were progressively overhauled and the Javelin radar units were removed, the bulky nose cone remaining in situ but with ballast installed to retain the aircraft's centre of gravity. Re-designated as the T.Mk.19, these Canberras joined No.85 Squadron at Binbrook, before returning to West Raynham to join No.100 Squadron. The final pair of active T.19s was assigned to No.7 Squadron at St.Mawgan and retired in 1980, these light and agile Canberras (that had started their lives as B.Mk.2 bombers) having been worked to the very end of their fatigue lives.

Whilst the Canberra Mk.12 and Mk.14 were export versions, the RAF's Canberra B.Mk.15 was a direct development of the B.Mk.6 airframe. With the B.Mk.6's integral wing tanks, uprated engines and underwing pylons, new radio equipment was also installed and an F95 camera was fitted in the nose, together with a G45 camera in the starboard wing leading edge. In most respects the Mk.15 was simply an uprated Mk.6 intended for operations in the Middle East and Far East, and the B.Mk.16 was the designation applied to similarly-modified B.Mk.6(BS) aircraft. The latter variant (assigned only to the Akrotiri Strike Wing) was a relatively short-lived sub-variant of the B.Mk.6 bomber, fitted with Blue Shadow

sideways-looking radar. Intended to provide navigational and target fixing information, Blue Shadow proved to be rather disappointing in terms of performance and it wasn't adopted for widespread use. Its sheer size also required the removal of one of the two rear cockpit ejection seats (the radar gear occupied much of the starboard seat's usual position), and if a second navigator and bomb aimer were carried, he was obliged to carry his own oxygen supply and parachute. The sideways radar system was a useful asset for a while, but as better systems emerged, the notion of equipping more Canberras soon seemed pointless, and no further aircraft were converted. The Canberra Mk.17 marked a significant transition away

The prototype Canberra T.Mk.22, WT510. Its new radome, taken from a Buccaneer, still retains its RAF camouflage. *(Photo: Tim McLelland collection)*

The Canberra T.Mk.22 was developed for the Royal Navy. A batch of seven was produced from redundant PR.Mk.7 airframes, the Blue Parrot radar being installed in a modified nose section including a Buccaneer radome. The T.Mk.22s were initially used for Buccaneer observer training but subsequently flew as threat simulators. They were often used as radar targets, acting as 'bombers', with a pair of FRADU Hunters flying in formation as 'missiles'. Operating from Yeovilton until 1984, the T.Mk.22s were replaced by a fleet of Dassault Falcon 20 business jets, suitably equipped for the same training role.
(Photos: BAC & Michael Freer)

Among the least well-known of RAF Canberra variants, the B.Mk.6(Mod) aircraft were flown by No.51 Squadron. Ostensibly assigned a 'signals' role, they were primarily operated as electronic intelligence-gatherers, equipped with a variety of sensors. The sensitive nature of their work means little detail is still available on them.
(Photos: Tim McLelland collection & Godfrey Mangion)

Canberra B.Mk.6 WH953 did not see service with the RAF, and went directly to the RAE for radar trials and development work. It was swiftly modified to carry a huge nose radome in which a variety of radar systems were tested, including systems destined for the Tornado programme. Like many RAE aircraft, it was repainted in 'Raspberry Ripple' red, white and blue colours during the 1980s. Following retirement the airframe was scrapped, although the cockpit and nose section is now preserved in Suffolk. *(Photo: Aeroplane)*

Canberra B.Mk.6 WT212 was used exclusively on test flying and research duties with the RAE and the Institute of Aviation Medicine. It was painted in an unusual livery comprising an overall white finish with red trim. The aircraft is pictured at RAF Valley during October 1972 just a year before it was withdrawn from use. *(Photo: Steve Williams)*

Canberra B.Mk.2 WK121 initially flew 'window' dropping trials at Defford, on loan from the RAF. It was then transferred to the RAE and eventually moved to Boscombe Down, where it was used on a variety of tasks including systems calibration and target facilities. During its time with the A&AEE it was painted in a very unusual scheme of white with pale blue trim, complete with pale national insignia. The purpose of these 'faded' markings remains unclear, since they were normally only applied to aircraft used in the strike role. Even more unusual was a subsequent change that saw black replace the white. Again, the purpose of the finish is unknown. *(Photos: Adrian Balch & Tim McLelland collection)*

from the type's role as a bomber and resulted in a specialised electronic countermeasures (ECM) and electronic warfare (EW) aircraft, assigned to a joint RAF and Fleet Air Arm squadron dedicated to the provision of ECM/EW training support. A batch of B.Mk.2 airframes was converted for the role, and although no major structural alterations were made to the fuselage, a completely new nose section was installed, housing ECM receiver and transmitter gear. Further ECM equipment was integrated into the bomb bay and into the tailcone and other modifications were made to the aircraft through its service life that continued until 1994 when No.360 Squadron disbanded.

The Canberra proved to be ideal for the EW role, acting as 'electronic enemy' for RAF and NATO aircraft on many routine training missions. Indeed, it was the introduction of the Tornado F.Mk.3 interceptor and trials with its new radar that took such a heavy toll on

No.360 Squadron's flying hours that the type's withdrawal had to be brought forward, simply because most of the T.Mk.17 fleet was literally worn out. But from all of the Canberra's exotic derivatives that gradually emerged, the T.Mk.17 has to be regarded as one of the most useful. The last major Canberra derivative to appear was the TT.Mk.18, a specialised target tug variant destined to replace Meteors in RAF and FAA service. By the mid-1960s Flight Refuelling Ltd had developed a new target and winch system for attachment to the Meteor, but the type's relatively small size meant that only one of the new Rushton target packs could be carried. The Canberra was quickly identified as a much more suitable aircraft for the Rushton winch and target, so conversion of a B.Mk.2 (WJ632) was undertaken by English Electric (now part of BAC). The conversion was successful and a standard conversion programme was

applied to 23 Canberra B.Mk.2 aircraft, all of which emerged from April 1970 onwards. Designated as the Canberra TT.Mk.18, the target tugs were assigned to the FAA at Yeovilton and to the RAF's No.7 Squadron at St Mawgan. They proved to be an invaluable asset for the RAF, FAA, and indeed the British Army, and although the last examples were withdrawn from RAF service during 1991, their retirement was a result of cost-cutting.

The RAF's Canberra fleet had first started to diminish in size when the V-Force gradually came into service. As more and more V-Bombers settled into service, the Canberra's shorter-range bombing capabilities were in effect redundant, and Bomber Command relinquished its last Canberra during 1961. However, the aircraft remained very much in the offensive bombing and attack business for many more years, with units in the Middle and Far East, and of course Germany. The Akrotiri Canberras returned home in 1969

(Photo: Aeroplane)

▲   Canberra B.Mk.6 WT309 was completed in May 1955 and immediately transferred to the Royal Aircraft Establishment as a trials and research platform. Unlike many RAE Canberras it was not extensively modified, receiving only a camera pod fairing on each wing tip. It operated primarily from Farnborough and went into storage there, pending disposal, during 1988. (Photo: FAST Museum)

Manufactured as a Canberra B.Mk.2 for the RAF, WJ638 served with Nos. 35 and 102 Squadrons before being withdrawn for conversion to U.10 unmanned drone configuration. It was operated by the Fleet Air Arm from Hal Far but survived intact and was transferred to the RRE at Pershore in 1961. It then went to the A&AEE at Boscombe Down where it was used as an ejection seat trials aircraft (above) until 1977 when it was withdrawn from use. WJ638 ended its days on the fire dump at Predannack. (Photo: Adrian Balch)

WH952 enjoyed a varied existence as a trials aircraft beginning in 1963 when it was used by the A&AEE for fatigue testing. It was then used to investigate bomb door buffet concerns before being re-assigned to weapons release testing. Its last active role was as a chase aircraft for the MRCA Tornado programme. It was retired and used for apprentice ground training at Bedford until 1982 when it was withdrawn. (Photo: Tim McLelland collection)

Canberra B.Mk.6 WT308 was used exclusively as a trials aircraft by the RAE after being transferred from RAF charge soon after delivery in 1955. Seen here at Farnborough shortly before its retirement in eye-catching 'Raspberry Ripple', the aircraft was withdrawn in 1988 and went to Predannack, where it has since languished as a training airframe, slowly succumbing to the attentions of fire crews. (Photo: FAST Museum)

Canberra B.Mk.6 XH568 was delivered to the RAE and was used in support of various programmes, including the Sea Skua missile. With the RRE at Pershore it was fitted with the radar nose taken from (retired) WG788 and remained in this configuration until its retirement. Purchased by a private owner it operated briefly on the civil register as a warbird but was subsequently used as a spares source (primarily for WT333 at Bruntingthorpe) and scrapped. (Photo: Aeroplane)

with aircraft from Singapore following a year later, but it wasn't until 1972 that the last Canberra B.Mk.(I)8 was withdrawn from RAF Germany, and this was the last year in which the RAF operated the aircraft in its designated bomber role.

But even this date was not to spell the end for this versatile and sturdy aircraft. Through the introduction of the many specialised training and support variants (and of course the continuing reconnaissance role), the Canberra remained in RAF service for many more years and it wasn't until July 2006 that the last Canberras (the aforementioned reconnaissance-equipped PR.Mk.9 aircraft) were finally withdrawn from use.

The Canberra's most deadly role as a nuclear-equipped strike aircraft based in Germany had contributed to NATO's strength through the darkest days of the Cold War, but thankfully the aircraft had never been called upon to deliver its deadly load. In fact, the Canberra's 55 years of active service saw very little 'real' action. It was only during the 1956 Suez Crisis that the Canberra saw front-line combat use, at the very beginning of its long operational life. Bomber Command's Canberras were deployed to

Malta and Cyprus as part of Operation Musketeer and bombing missions were launched against many targets inside Egypt, including airfields. But the Canberra's effectiveness during the crisis as a bomber was a huge disappointment to service chiefs, not because of any deficiencies with either the aircraft or its crews, but because of the equipment and support given to the aircraft. With only Gee-H as its main navigational aid, the Canberra crews had to rely on traditional map-reading to locate their targets, simply because Gee-H was useless without the ground beacons needed to generate homing signals.

Resorting to bombing techniques that had been used in World War Two was both a frustration and an embarrassment, especially when the Canberra was clearly such a capable aeroplane. The handful of converted Canberra B.Mk.6(BS) aircraft equipped with Blue Shadow radar were employed during the crisis as target markers for both the Canberra and Valiant bomber forces that performed attacks on Egypt, but without any up-to-date reconnaissance images of their targets, the Canberra radar operators had nothing to which they could compare their relatively poor radar pictures.

Despite this, Bomber Command achieved some satisfactory results, but Suez demonstrated graphically that the Canberra's outstanding flying qualities had to be matched by good navigational and bombing equipment, and supported with all of the necessary target information. It was a lesson that the RAF learned well, and as a direct result of Suez, the Canberra and V-Force was supported by a much stronger and practical infrastructure.

The Canberra paved the way for the RAF's V-Force squadrons and gave NATO a fearsome strike capability poised virtually on the USSR's doorstep. Almost as an unexpected bonus it also provided the RAF with a versatile and reliable aircraft that readily lent itself to a whole range of support and training tasks. It is quite ironic to note how the majority of the Canberra's long RAF career was actually occupied by duties that had very little to do with the bombing role for which it had been designed and manufactured. After more than half a century of active use, nobody could deny that the Canberra had been anything other than an outstanding jet bomber – especially when one considers that it had of course, been Britain's very first one. ❖

Canberra T.Mk.17 WJ607. No.360 Squadron, 1977. Dark Sea Grey and
Dark Green disruptive camouflage with Light Aircraft Grey
undersides. Red and blue national insignia and black serials. Unit
emblem on tail with white codes.

Canberra T.Mk.17A WD955. No.360 Squadron 1994. Aircraft is
painted in Hemp with Light Aircraft Grey undersides. National
insignia is pale "pink and lilac" with white serials and codes. Unit
colours are applied to the tail and fuselage sides in red and yellow.

Canberra B.Mk.6 WT309. Aeroplane & Armament Experimental
Establishment, Boscombe Down 1990. Aircraft wears standard
MoD(PE) colours comprising of Oxford Blue undersides with white
upper surfaces, and Signal Red trim. The "Apprentice Training" titling
was applied to the aircraft after it was withdrawn from flying duties.

Canberra U.Mk.10 WH876, Aeroplane & Armament Experimental
Establishment, Boscombe Down, 1983. Light Aircraft Grey and white
finish with black and white photographic calibration markings. Post
Office Red trip on tail and wing tips. A bolt-on refuelling probe was
occasionally fitted to this aircraft, ahead of the cockpit canopy.

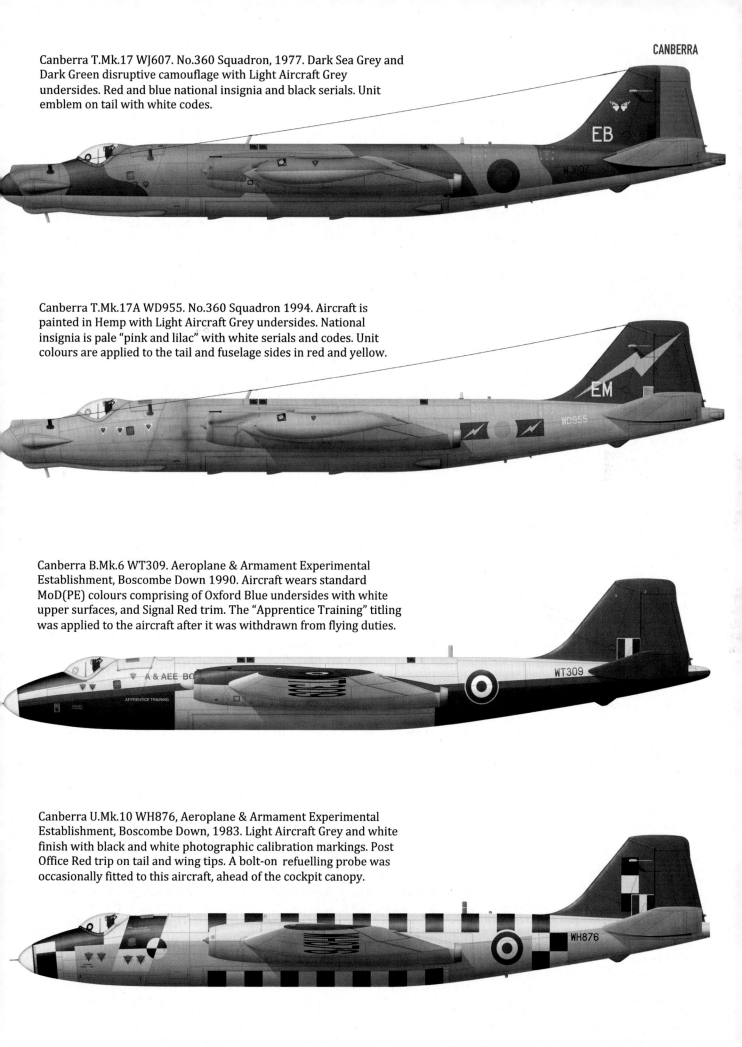

Drawings by Chris Sandham-Bailey (www.inkworm.co.uk)

EXPORT EXCELLENCE

The Canberra's worldwide international sales record was impressive. Adoption by the United States was remarkable

The first production standard B-57A Canberra produced by Martin, 52-1418 was pictured over Chesapeake Bay shortly after its maiden flight. Although virtually identical to the Canberra B.Mk.2, the modified nacelles for the American J65 engines are clearly visible. *(Photo: Tim McLelland collection)*

A busy scene at Middle River, Baltimore, with countless B-57A Canberras on Martin's production line, as a completed aircraft is rolled out for flight testing. *(Photo: Tim McLelland collection)*

One of the Canberra's most notable achievements was its effective export to the United States, where the type was built under licence as the B-57. With a huge aerospace industry at their disposal, America's air arms inevitably relied on indigenous designs and by the late 1940s the North American B-45 was already being produced for the USAF.

The Korean War soon demonstrated that the USAF needed a medium jet bomber that was capable of operating in the night intruder role and a variety of existing designs were swiftly examined, including the B-45 and other types such as the AJ-1 Savage and the Martin XB-51 that was under development. The USAF needed a suitable aircraft as quickly as possible and although it was anticipated that an American type would be chosen for immediate production, the Canberra was also considered, not least because of the dazzling performance of the prototype at Farnborough that had captivated everyone, including a number of American observers.

A party of American officials requested an evaluation of the Canberra and English Electric arranged for a demonstration to be made at the huge USAF base at Burtonwood, just a few minutes' flying time from Warton. On 17 August 1950 test pilot Roland Beamont duly arrived at Burtonwood in the second Canberra prototype VX169, making a brief engines-running stop to enable VIPs to examine the interior and exterior of the aircraft. Then, in foul weather conditions, Beamont proceeded to get airborne in just 2,000ft and immediately performed a neat climbing roll before embarking on a short demonstration that culminated in a fast and low pass over the runway. The officials were impressed and a few weeks later they visited Warton to examine the Canberra in more detail. It quickly became clear to English Electric that the USAF wanted to acquire the Canberra, and a tentative agreement was made to supply a batch of 300 aircraft drawn from projected RAF production, pending the delivery of larger numbers of American B-51 aircraft. However, in order to make a definitive choice, the USAF arranged a fly-off at Andrews AFB and on 21 February 1951 the fourth production Canberra (WD932) was ferried to the States via Aldergrove and Gander and on 26 February Beamont prepared to display the aircraft before an assembled crowd of officials and VIPs. A set

Canberra B.Mk.2 WD940, repainted as B-57A 51-17352 outside Martin's Baltimore factory. The standard Bomber Command grey and black colours were retained but USAF serials and insignia were applied. Traces of the British national insignia are still visible on the wing upper surfaces. *(Photo: Tim McLelland collection)*

▲ ➤   Two magnificent images of the first production B-57A 52-1418 taken after roll-out, and just moments after take-off on its maiden flight on 20 July 1953. As can be seen, wing tip fuel tanks were removed for the first flight, and a large sensor boom was attached to the port wing tip – this was common to many pre-production and trials B-57As.
(Photos: Tim McLelland collection)

routine of manoeuvres was laid down for the competing aircraft, including the Canberra, XB-51, and B-45, and it was stipulated that each aircraft should complete precisely the same sequence so that a comparative evaluation could be made.

Roland Beamont was allocated the final display slot, and after the XB-51 completed its performance, he took WD932 into the air and repeated the routine. In comparison to the preceding aircraft the Canberra was immediately seen to be more agile, with all of the set manoeuvres being completed within the airfield boundary. After finishing, Beamont realised that he still had another four minutes of allocated display time at his disposal, so he aborted his landing and hauled the Canberra into a tight 360⁰ turn before completing a half-roll into a fast and low flypast over the runway. He then pulled up into a high wingover and shut down both engines prior to entering a spiral descent into a short landing. The spectators were spellbound, and failed to notice that when the aircraft touched down the main tyres burst, thanks to the abrasive white sand surface that had just been applied to the runway. But with the landing still under full control, everyone's attention was still on the spectacle that had just unfolded.

After a series of dull and laborious demonstrations, the sprightly Canberra was in a completely different category. The XB-51 was undoubtedly faster than the Canberra in a straight line, but with high wing loading it was no match for the supremely capable Canberra, and thanks to Beamont's awe-inspiring demonstration there was no doubt as to what choice should be made – the Canberra won by a mile.

Ironically, the Glenn L. Martin company (that had produced the XB-51) was selected to manufacture the Canberra under license, chiefly because it had few other orders at that time. The US had taken the rare step of adopting a foreign military design for its air force, and an order for 250 aircraft designated B-57A was placed. Two DC-4 flights transported a massive quantity of English Electric manufacturing drawings to the Martin plant and WD932 was handed over as a pattern aircraft, serial 51-17387. The aircraft was destroyed on 21 December 1951 after being flown beyond its centre-of-gravity limits in a tight turn (the forward fuel tanks had been selected first, thereby placing excessive stresses on the wing structure). A second pattern aircraft (WD940) was delivered to Martin eight months later. It was used to develop a number of changes to the Canberra airframe, some made in order

to improve the aircraft's capability, while others were in response to a lingering perception that the aircraft was less safe and reliable than it could be, prompted by the loss of WD932. Of course, the Canberra was already a very satisfactory machine, but many American officials couldn't help feeling that despite its outstanding performance, it must have somehow been less than perfect without American know-how. Eventually, just eight B-57As were produced, followed by the main production version in the shape of the RB-57A, a combined reconnaissance and bomber platform with a camera installation fitted to the rear of the bomb bay. Although largely similar to the RAF's Canberra B.Mk.2, the B-57A and RB-57A did exhibit some obvious differences, not least the reshaped engine nacelles that now housed a pair of J65 turbojets, license-produced versions of the British Sapphire engine, manufactured by Buick and Wright. Additionally, the Canberra's unique 'finger' air brakes on the upper and lower wings were replaced by much more effective air brake doors that extended from the rear fuselage. The first USAF operator of the aircraft was the 363rd Tactical Reconnaissance Wing at Shaw AFB, where the first aircraft entered service during the summer of 1954.

RB-57A 52-1447 was assigned to the 363rd Tactical Reconnaissance Wing. This unit was the first to attain operational capability on the RB-57, and reached this status late in 1954 at Shaw AFB in South Carolina. Markings were in red, with red/white unit markings on the tail. *(Photo: Tim McLelland collection)*

▲ B-57B 52-1493 was initially used for flight testing before being permanently modified to NB-57B standard for operational trials. It was used to evaluate guidance system equipment for the Bomarc missile and withdrawn from use in 1961. It was stored at the Aircraft Maintenance and Regeneration Center (AMARC) at Davis-Monthan AFB until 1964 when It was dismantled. *(Photo: Tim McLelland collection)*

Its natural metal finish heavily weathered, B-57B 53-3908 was with the 405th FW. The aircraft was lost to ground fire a few weeks after this photograph was taken. Both crew were killed when it came down near Hao Chu Hi Mountain in South Vietnam. *(Photo: Tim McLelland collection)*

Pictured during a visit to Prestwick in 1957, B-57B 53-3954 served with the 461st TBG and 345th TBG until 1959, when the aircraft was refurbished and sold to Pakistan, where it joined No.31 Bomber Wing at Masroor AB. *(Photo: Tim McLelland collection)*

B-57C 53-3849 was delivered to the USAF in 1964 and joined the 8th BS of the 405th FW. A year later it was transferred to the South Vietnamese Air Force but after only a few months it was returned to the manufacturer for structural wing repairs. It then joined the 4424th Combat Crew Training Squadron (CCTS) and continued to fly until 1972 when it was placed in storage at AMARC. It was scrapped a few years later on site. *(Photo: Tim McLelland collection)*

Another Vietnam casualty was B-57C 53-3836. Assigned to the 3rd BW, it crashed during a training mission near Clark AFB, with the loss of both crew, in June 1964. The unusual kangaroo emblem on the aircraft's tail was presumably applied by an Australian Canberra crew. The B-57C was a combat-capable dual control variant of the B-57B airframe. (Photo: Tim McLelland collection)

Assigned to the 8th BS (405th FW), B-57B 53-3895 served in southeast Asia during the Vietnam conflict. It crashed in June 1965 while on approach to Da Nang AB, after suffering a wing fire. Both crew were killed. (Photo: Tim McLelland collection)

This panoramic view of Osan AB was taken in 1960. It shows the huge quantities of smoke expelled by the B-57's engine cartridge starters — even more than normally produced by its British equivalents. (Photo: Tim McLelland collection)

The B-57B was a direct development of the early American Canberra variant, and it incorporated many more modifications that were deemed necessary to equip the aircraft for USAF operations. Most notably, the entire forward fuselage was redesigned to incorporate a new two-man crew tandem seating arrangement, under a one-piece hinged canopy, combined with a conventional windscreen. The new nose section was attached to the existing Canberra airframe and enabled Martin to abandon the rather unusual (and typically British) crew layout employed in RAF machines, and the B-57A. The troublesome bubble canopy was gone and with tandem seating there was now excellent all-round visibility for both the pilot and navigator. Additionally, the conventional windscreen enabled a gunsight to be added, and ejection seats for both crew members could be fitted easily. Just as importantly, the bomb bay doors were replaced by a new revolving door that avoided the buffeting effects that were exhibited when the standard Canberra doors were opened. The one-piece door was designed as a removable component so that it could be loaded with bombs and swiftly installed between missions so that a rapid turnaround rate could be achieved. Underwing hardpoints were also fitted and both cannon and machine guns could be installed inside the wing structure. These modifications - combined with various other improvements to the aircraft's systems - created an aeroplane that was undoubtedly superior to the standard Canberra, and it is surprising that neither English Electric nor the Air Staff showed any interest in incorporating them into Canberra models being produced for

the RAF. The USAF was more than satisfied with the B-57B and it became an important and useful asset during the Vietnam conflict, where aircraft were employed on bombing, attack, reconnaissance and other types of missions. The first B-57s to be deployed to South Vietnam were not operated in an offensive role. The need for additional reconnaissance assets (particularly those with night capability) led to the deployment of two RB-57E aircraft in 1963. B-57Bs from the 8th and 13th Bomb Squadrons arrived at Bien Hoa in August 1964. Low-level missions designated as training flights were first conducted with the intention of creating a psychological effect on enemy forces, but the first combat sortie was flown on 19 February 1965 and the first excursion into North Vietnam took place on 2 March as part of Operation Rolling Thunder. For these missions, the aircraft typically carried nine

500lb bombs in its bomb bay and four 750lb bombs under the wings. In April, B-57s began flying night intruder missions supported by flare ships and electronic warfare aircraft. B-57s were primarily used for dive-bombing and strafing, early models carrying eight machine guns, four per wing, while later models mounted four 20mm cannon, two per wing. These weapons, combined with the bomb loads and up to four hours of flight time, made the B-57B an ideal ground support aircraft, and exceptional 'truck killer' along the Ho Chi Minh trail. Due to combat attrition, the B-57Bs were transferred to Phan Rang in October 1966 where they supported operations in the Iron Triangle along with Australian Canberra B.Mk.20s. The aircraft also continued to fly night interdiction missions against the Ho Chi Minh trail. Of the 94 B-57Bs deployed to southeast Asia, 51

Built for target towing, the B-57E was essentially a specialised version of the dual-control B-57C. Fighter aircraft equipped with 2.75in 'Mighty Mouse' air-to-air rockets practised against towed targets trailing almost a mile behind the B-57E, while some B-57Es were modified to deploy two bomb-shaped targets made from Styrofoam. Coated in radar-reflective paint, these were used for radar intercept live fire training. The targets were lightweight and generated significantly less drag than the huge cloth target, allowing the B-57E to reach up to 40,000ft with the target fully extended. The B-57E was retired from target towing in the early 1960s, when unguided rockets gave way to guided air-to-air missiles. In the mid-1960s, 12 such aircraft were converted as bombers and transferred to Vietnam. *(Photos: USAF)*

The EB–57 conversions were EW 'aggressors'. They used electronic jamming equipment and chaff released from dispensers on their wing pylons during training exercises against US and Canadian radar stations and interceptors. Air defence ground controllers were tasked with identifying the incoming EB-57 and directing jets to intercept. The EB-57A, EB-57B and EB-57E employed increasingly sophisticated threat simulation equipment and USAF and ANG units flew them into the 1980s. Aircraft 55-4247 was an EB-57E; the '0' prefix to the serial presentation on its tail indicates an airframe over ten years old or otherwise considered obsolete.
(Photos: Tim McLelland collection and USAF)

were eventually lost in combat and seven other Canberras to other causes. Only nine were still flying by 1969.

B-57s returned to southeast Asia in the form of the B-57G, deployed to Thailand during the autumn of 1970. Intended as a night intruder to help combat movement along the Ho Chi Minh trail, these aircraft were equipped with a variety of new sensors, and were capable of dropping laser-guided munitions. One B-57G was modified to house an Emerson TAT-161 turret with a single M61 20mm cannon in its bomb bay, acting as a gunship under project Pave Gat. After delays in testing at Eglin AFB, Florida, Pave Gat tests proved that "the B-57G could hit stationary or moving targets with its 20mm gun, day or night. Loaded with 4,000 rounds of ammunition, the Pave Gat B-57G could hit as many as 20 targets, three times as many as the bomb-carrying B-57G. The Pave

Gat aircraft could avoid antiaircraft fire by firing from offset positions, while the bomb carrier had to pass directly over the target." Deployment to the region was resisted, however, as the decision had been made in August 1971 to return the B-57G squadron to the US early in 1972, leaving insufficient evaluation time. The B-57G was finally withdrawn from Thailand in May 1972.

The B-57 soldiered on in USAF service long after Vietnam, and the basic B-57 airframe was developed into a variety of specialised versions, including the aforementioned B-57G with a laser-designation system in its nose, and the EB-57A/B electronic 'aggressor' aircraft. Most significantly, it was developed as a dedicated reconnaissance platform, notably as the RB-57D high-altitude aircraft, incorporating a completely new outer wing design of increased span and chord, enabling the

aircraft to reach 70,000ft. This design was developed still further, resulting in the RB-57F, with an even larger wing structure and new turbofan engines. This allowed the aircraft to reach altitudes of more than 82,000ft, and it became a very useful reconnaissance asset in the USAF's inventory. However, the huge wings suffered from fatigue cracking and both the RB-57D and RB-57F began to exhibit stress fractures after only a few years' service. The high cost of repairs ultimately led to the types' withdrawal. It wasn't surprising that NASA showed a great interest in the 'big wing' Canberra, and even after all B-57's had finally been retired from USAF and Air National Guard service in the 1970s, a handful of these specialised Canberra derivatives continued to fly on a variety of scientific research duties. Rather more surprising was that in 2011 a WB-57F was brought back into use after

Some B-57Cs were modified for alternative missions during the 1960s under a variety of designations – the aircraft illustrated above and below were both to WB-57C standard. At least one WB-57C, 53-3944, was used during Project Clean Sweep III to gather data from inside nuclear fallout clouds. It launched a sampling rocket from around 30,000ft after pitching nose-up to between 55° and 60°. The rocket climbed to about 100,000ft, where it penetrated the clouds and began collecting air samples and other data. *(Photos: USAF)*

The B-57 first deployed to South Vietnam is response to an urgent need for reconnaissance assets, especially those capable of operating at night. An initial two RB-57Es deployed for operations beginning on 7 May 1963. Project Patricia Lynn modified six B-57Es with optical and infra-red sensors to create the RB-57E. In August 1965, an RB-57F was deployed to Udon Royal Thai Airforce Base under Projects Greek God and Mad King but failed to gather the hoped-for intelligence on North Vietnamese SAM sites. The effort was terminated in October, but Project Sky Wave saw another RB-57F attempt a similar mission in December 1965, with similarly poor results; it was withdrawn in February 1966. *(Photo: USAF)*

▲

Compared to the standard B-57, the RB-57D's wing was increased in span — to 106ft — and chord, creating a high-aspect ratio wing suited to the aircraft's high-altitude reconnaissance role. Pratt & Whitney J57 engines, each producing almost 6,000lb more thrust than the J65, were installed, and the B-57's standard fuselage fuel tanks removed in favour of wing fuel cells. A variable-incidence, all-moving tailplane replaced the regular unit, and spoilers on the outer wings assisted the ailerons in roll control. Twenty RB-57Ds were built in four versions, the type entering service in 1956, pending the introduction of the U-2. The long wing caused serious structural problems and after an accident in 1964 the fleet was withdrawn. A rebuild programme in 1966 returned some aircraft to service, however, before the last was retired in 1970. No more than three RB-57Ds were transferred to Taiwan in 1958. They flew until 1964, by which time one had been lost to a Soviet SAM. *(Photo: USAF)*

◄

The RB-57F added an even larger wing than that of the RB-57D to an existing B-57 fuselage. Pratt & Whitney TF33 turbofan engines provided more than twice the thrust available to a B-57B and a podded J60 turbojet could be mounted under each wing. Capable of reaching 82,000ft, these aircraft provided the USAF with a useful reconnaissance capability but, as with the RB-57D, the wing structure proved susceptible to fatigue cracking and the RB-57F had been withdrawn by 1974. *(Photo: Tim McLelland collection)*

having been placed in external storage for more than 40 years. In 2013, this brought NASA's Canberra fleet back up to three WB-57Fs. Operated from Ellington Field, Texas they are the last operational Canberras.

SUCCESS BEYOND THE US

Following the success of the Canberra with the USAF, English Electric (which became part of the British Aircraft Corporation, now BAE Systems) produced a considerable number of Canberras for other countries. Perhaps most appropriately, Australia showed great interest in the aircraft from the outset and by the time of the aircraft's ceremonial naming at Biggin Hill in January 1951, a contract with Australia had been signed and two aircraft (WD939 and WD983) were ferried to Amberley, where they enabled RAAF crews to train on the type. License production in Australia

was undertaken by Government Aircraft Factories (GAF), the first aircraft making its maiden flight on 29 May 1953. Australia's Mk.20 was virtually identical to the RAF's B.Mk.2 although internal wing fuel tanks (as in the B.Mk.6) were fitted, and different navigational and radio equipment was installed. Unlike the RAF, navigating and bomb aiming was undertaken by the same crewman, and so only two crew were carried. Some 48 aircraft were manufactured, replacing a fleet of elderly Avro Lincolns, and seven dual-control Mk.21 trainers were also produced. Like the USAF, the RAAF operated its Canberras in Vietnam and the type remained in use until the early 1980s, by which stage only a handful were still active, assigned to the Aircraft Research and Development Unit (ARDU) at Edinburgh.

Argentina placed a contract for Canberras late in 1967 and ten B.Mk.62 aircraft were ordered together with a pair of B.Mk.64

trainers (these being export equivalents of the B.Mk.2 and T.Mk.4). Deliveries began late in 1970, and a further pair of aircraft (a T.Mk.94 and B.Mk.92) was ordered in 1981. However, both were subsequently cancelled when the Falklands conflict began. Argentina employed its Canberras early in the war following the RAF's first Vulcan raid, but after being intercepted by FAA Sea Harriers (one aircraft was shot down), the Canberras didn't reappear until late in the war, when night bombing raids against British forces were conducted. Another Canberra was shot down by a Sea Dart missile fired from HMS *Exeter*, which marked the end of the Canberra's involvement in the conflict, during which some 35 missions had been flown, dropping around 100,000lb of bombs in the process. By the end of 1982 only five Canberras remained in active use, and these remained in use for a few more years until the type was finally retired.

NASA has operated several Canberras in different variants. Some were assigned to flight testing for the B-57 programme, others used extensively in a wide range of projects for weapons systems, flight controls, atmospheric research, and other areas of interest. The 'standard' B-57B found its way into NASA service with various degrees of modification. The aircraft shown at the bottom of the page flew high-altitude missions assessing the capacity of solar cells in support of the space programme. NASA 809 also flew space-related missions, but only while its mission suite was in development. Its work on the Viking Mars lander project over, it received its originally intended modifications, equipping it to gather atmospheric data and, later, information on airflow around mountains and in the jet stream, and on convective and clear air turbulence. *(Photos: NASA)*

Latterly redesignated as the WB-57F, the RB-57F was subject to a limited wing repair programme that ultimately proved financially prohibitive. Back in 1968, NASA borrowed a USAF RB-57F for its Earth Resources Technology Satellite (ERTS) programme, taking ownership of the aircraft in 1972, as NASA 925. Two more WB-57Fs were added as NASA 926 and NASA 928, before 925 was retired in 1982. The fleet was brought back up to three when another WB-57F was removed from desert storage and restored as NASA 927, for a return to flight on 9 August 2013. Early in 2024, all three aircraft remained available, based at Ellington Field, alongside the Johnson Space Center, in Houston, Texas.

(Photos: NASA)

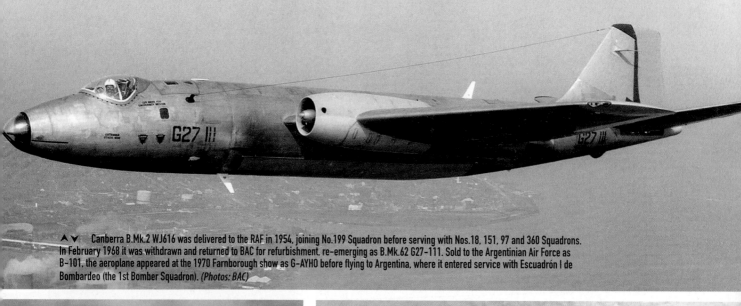

▲▼ Canberra B.Mk.2 WJ616 was delivered to the RAF in 1954, joining No.199 Squadron before serving with Nos.18, 151, 97 and 360 Squadrons. In February 1968 it was withdrawn and returned to BAC for refurbishment, re-emerging as B.Mk.62 G27-111. Sold to the Argentinian Air Force as B-101, the aeroplane appeared at the 1970 Farnborough show as G-AYHO before flying to Argentina, where it entered service with Escuadrón I de Bombardeo (the 1st Bomber Squadron). *(Photos: BAC)*

The Falklands saga eventually resulted in Chile becoming a customer for the Canberra, although the precise details of this export process remain shrouded in mystery. It is known that Chile provided direct support to Britain during the conflict and it is thought that RAF reconnaissance Canberras operated from Chile, despite the refusal of British authorities to confirm or deny this. After the conflict ended, three former RAF Canberra PR.Mk.9s were withdrawn from storage at St Athan and returned to their former home at Wyton, where Chilean crews trained on the aircraft before flying them to Los Carrillos near Santiago. They were operated for only a few years, one aircraft being lost in an accident in May 1983. Although no official details of these Canberras have so far been released, it seems likely that the three aircraft were simply given to Chile in exchange for the vital assistance that was given to British forces during the Falklands campaign.

Ecuador ordered six B.Mk.6 Canberras in May 1954, taken from the existing line of B.Mk.6s that were being manufactured for the RAF. Delivered in 1955, the aircraft remained in service until the mid-1980s, although by this stage only three remained active. They all returned to Britain for

refurbishment at Samlesbury during their service lives, one example suffering a technical problem, forcing an unscheduled landing at Ballykelly, with the rest of its journey being completed on board an Irish ferry.

Ethiopia acquired four refurbished Canberra B.Mk.2s, designated as the B.Mk.52 and intended for the counter-insurgency role. Completed in 1968, the aircraft were all delivered by the end of that year. Little is known about Ethiopia's Canberra operations, although with poor technical support, the aircraft were often unfit to fly and their operational use was rather short-lived. One aircraft was damaged in a landing accident (but may have been repaired) and another was lost to an undisclosed Arab state when its pilot defected, taking the Canberra with him. It is believed that the other two aircraft were destroyed during a conflict with Somalia.

Rather nearer to home, France also showed some interest in it, although there was no stated intention to adopt the aircraft for operational use within the French Air Force. Instead, it was the Centre d'Essais en Vol (CEV) and Centre du Tir et de Bombardement (CTB) that acquired a total of

six, all manufactured to B.Mk.6 standard. They were delivered in 1955 and were used for a wide variety of trials work including weapons and radar systems testing. At least one was subsequently fitted with a B.Mk.8 forward fuselage (complete with fighter-type cockpit), and one was also used as an engine test bed. They remained active into the late 1970s and one example was retained for display at Le Bourget, suggesting that despite its foreign origins, the French were suitably impressed by this all-British product.

India was a particularly significant export customer for the Canberra, obtaining new-build aircraft and the Canberra became the backbone of the Indian Air Force for bombing raids and photo-reconnaissance operations for many years. Negotiations to acquire the Canberra as a replacement for the short-lived and obsolete B-24 Liberator began in 1954. During the extended negotiations between Britain and India, the Soviet Union is alleged to have offered the Ilyushin Il-28, at a significantly lower price. However, in January 1957 India placed a large order for the Canberra, comprising a total of 54 B(I).Mk.58 bombers, eight PR.Mk.57 photo-reconnaissance aircraft, and six T.Mk.4 training aircraft, deliveries beginning

Argentina's Canberra force comprised 10 Canberra B.Mk.62 bombers and a pair of T.Mk.64 trainers. They were used during the 1982 Falklands conflict (as illustrated) and remained in use until 2000. *(Photo: Tim McLelland collection)*

▲ ⌄ The first Australian-built Canberra completed its maiden flight on 29 May 1953 and the type entered service with the RAAF in December 1953. Deployed to Malaysia and Vietnam, Australia's Canberras proved versatile and effective, armed with free-fall bombs, machine guns and cannon. As the F-111 entered service the RAAF Canberra fleet slowly wound down, the last being withdrawn in 1982.
(Photos: Tim McLelland collection)

▲ Chile was not a major operator of the Canberra, but after having assisted British forces during the 1982 Falklands conflict, three former RAF Canberra PR.Mk.9 aircraft were supplied to the country, possibly as a gift in exchange for the (undisclosed) support given to Britain.
(Photo: Tim McLelland collection)

The RNZAF purchased 11 B(I).Mk.12 and two T.Mk.13 Canberras to replace Vampire attack aircraft. Delivered between 1959 and 1961, they were assigned to No.14 Squadron and the Bomber Conversion Unit. Three Canberras were lost in RNZAF service, including a loaned RAF machine (WF915) lost in severe turbulence in October 1961; NZ6101, which crashed in November 1960 after losing power on approach to Christchurch International; and NZ6104, which crashed into the sea near Singapore in November 1964. The survivors were withdrawn from service in July 1970, replaced by the A-4K Skyhawk. Canberra NZ6106 was sold back to BAC and the remainder to the Indian Air Force.
(Photos: Tim McLelland collection)

▲ Ethiopia bought four refurbished B.Mk.2s, with an expected second order never materialising. Serving in such small numbers, the aircraft's operational usefulness was limited. One was destroyed in a landing accident, another lost when a pilot defected, and the remainder are believed to have been destroyed by Cuban mercenary pilots flying MiG-21s. *(Photo: Tim McLelland collection)*

▲ In 1959, 24 B-57B and two B-57C aircraft from the inactivated 345th Tactical Bomber Group at Langley AFB, Virginia, were ferried to Mauripur AB in Karachi, Pakistan to form the 7th and 8th Bomber Squadrons of the 31st Bomber Wing of the Pakistan Air Force. From 1963, the Pakistani B-57Bs were retrofitted with the RB-1A all-weather bombing system, giving them a longer nose profile than the standard B-57B. Some also received underwing hardpoints for four fuel tanks, providing sufficient range to reach targets well inside India. The B-57Bs remained in service until 1985, when they were replaced by F-16A Fighting Falcons. *(Photo: PAF)*

▲ Fifteen Canberra B.Mk.2 bombers were obtained from Britain during 1959 and flown out to Rhodesia from June 1959, followed by a further three T.Mk.4 trainers in March 1961. Used by No.5 Squadron for many years, they were gradually withdrawn as they reached the end of their fatigue lives. Two aircraft were constructed from cannibalised spares taken from grounded aircraft, and two additional aircraft (a B.Mk.2 and one Mk.4 were supplied from Britain in 1981. They were all withdrawn late in 1983.

in the summer of that same year. A total of 12 more Canberras was ordered in September 1957, and at least 30 more had been purchased by 1962. First used in combat by the IAF in 1962, the Canberra was employed during the UN campaign against the breakaway Republic of Katanga in Africa. During the Indo-Pakistani Wars of the 1960s and 1970s, the type was used by both sides. The most audacious use of the bomber was during the Second Kashmir War, when the Indian Air Force sent in its Canberras to attack a critical Pakistani radar post in West Pakistan. The raid was a complete success, the radars in Badin having been badly damaged by the bombing and put out of commission. A later raid by the IAF was attempted on Peshawar air base with the aim of destroying, amongst other targets, several Pakistani B-57 bombers, but due to poor visibility, a road outside of the base was bombed instead of the runway where the

PAF B-57s were parked. During the Indo-Pakistani War of 1971, Indian Canberras flew a strategically important sortie against Karachi oil tanks, helping the Indian Navy in its own operations, a series of missile boat attacks against the Pakistani coast. On 21 May 1999, prior to the Kargil War, the Indian Air Force Air assigned a PR.Mk.57 aircraft on a photographic mission near the Line of Control, where it took a severe blow from a FIM-92 Stinger infra-red homing missile on the starboard engine; the Canberra successfully returned to base using just one engine. The entire Indian Air Force Canberra fleet was grounded following the crash of an IAF Canberra in December 2005, although the aircraft remained active on second-line duties (particularly the provision of target facilities) until final retirement in May 2007.

➤ West Germany purchased three former RAF Canberra B.Mk.2s for research and experimental use. Delivered in 1966, the aircraft were eventually repainted in a bright orange paint scheme. Civil registrations were eventually exchanged for standard Luftwaffe codes. One aircraft suffered a wheels-up landing and was rebuilt with wings from former RAF Canberra TT.Mk.18 WK123.

▲ Venezuela was an enthusiastic Canberra customer, placing numerous orders over many years and using the aircraft as a high- and low-altitude bomber and in the close support role. Much of the fleet was returned to the UK for refurbishment and at least one aircraft was refurbished twice, before Venezuela assumed responsibility for its own Canberra overhaul procedures under BAC approval. *(Photos: BAC)*

▲ Peru operated a relatively large and varied fleet of Canberras, the first being delivered in 1956. Canberra operations continued for almost half a decade, the type making its final flight in Peruvian service in 2003. Several airframes remained in open storage into 2016, after which they were disposed of or abandoned. *(Photo: Chris Lofting)*

Six Canberra B(I).Mk.12s were exported to South Africa, together with three Canberra T.Mk.4 trainers. They were all operated by the SAAF's No. 12 Squadron, and they saw action on various occasions, including strike missions against Angolan and Zambian forces. They remained active until 1990 when they were placed in storage. A few aircraft were sold to Peru while the rest were retained for preservation. *(Photo: Tim McLelland collection)*

New Zealand first acquired Canberras on loan from the RAF, equipping the RNZAF's No.75 Squadron in support of the ongoing Malaysian campaign, in which both RAF and RNZAF aircraft were heavily involved. An order for 11 Canberras (nine Mk.8 interdictors and two Mk.4 trainers) was placed early in 1958. These, together with the aircraft provided on a loan basis, were used operationally until 1970 at which stage New Zealand retired its Canberra fleet, the majority being sold to India. Peru also ordered the Canberra, starting with a batch of eight Mk.8 aircraft followed by a single attrition replacement. A third contract covered six former B.Mk.2 aircraft and a pair of former RAF T.Mk.4s, a fourth contract for six aircraft assembled from various former B.Mk.2 airframes, a fifth and sixth for single attrition replacements, followed by a seventh order comprising 11 Mk.8 variants. These were re-manufactured by Marshalls at Cambridge, as BAC was by this stage (1973) committed to production and testing of the new MRCA, later the Tornado. Peru continued to operate a dwindling fleet of Canberras until July 2002 when the remaining handful of operational aircraft was withdrawn, although they were stored in 'flyable' condition for some time. Rhodesia

ordered 15 former RAF B.Mk.2 Canberras in 1957, followed by a further three aircraft in 1958. All were in service by 1961, and although little is known about Rhodesian Canberra operations, they were used operationally in counter-terrorist operations and remained active into the 1980s, by which stage a surviving fleet of 11 aircraft was transferred to the new air force of Zimbabwe. South Africa's association with the Canberra began in 1963 when the first of six new-build B(I).Mk.12 aircraft were delivered to SAAF No.12 Squadron. They were employed in an ongoing conflict along the Namibian and Angolan borders and remained operational until 1990. Three former RAF T.Mk.4 aircraft were delivered in 1963 and in 1991 a batch of five MK.12 aircraft was sold to Peru, the rest remaining in use until 1991 when the Canberra fleet was withdrawn and placed in storage as part of the country's reduction in defence spending.

Further exports were made to Sweden, where two aircraft were supplied for radar and avionics trials work with F 8 Wing. These former B.Mk.2 aircraft were delivered in 1960 and they were operated until 1973. Three Canberras were supplied to West Germany, likewise assigned to test flying. Ordered in

1965, the three former B.Mk.2 aircraft joined Erprobungsstelle 61 during 1966, initially with civilian registrations that were later exchanged for standard Luftwaffe codes. They remained in use into the 1990s, one aircraft (99+34) suffering a wheels-up landing that prompted the purchase of former RAF TT.Mk.18 WK123, from which the wings were removed and fitted to the German aircraft. Finally (although it was in fact the very first export customer) Venezuela also purchased Canberras, with an order being placed in 1953 for six B.Mk.2s. A second contract placed in 1957 covered ten Mk.8 airframes and a pair of Mk.4 trainers, while a further 14 refurbished aircraft (12 Mk.2s and two PR.Mk.3s) were purchased in 1965. The last operational examples were believed to have been withdrawn from use during the 1990s. By any standards, the Canberra's export record was impressive, not least because the aircraft was a relatively expensive and sophisticated bomber aircraft that was designed primarily for the RAF's requirements. But it was undoubtedly America's decision to buy into the Canberra and build the B-57 that secured the aircraft's place in history as a very significant warplane of its era. ❖

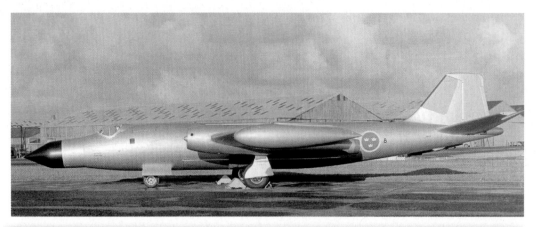

Sweden acquired two former RAF Canberra B.Mk.2s, for airborne testing of radar and avionics equipment. They were fitted with T.Mk.19-type radomes and designated as the TP 52 in Swedish service, although they were inevitably referred to as Canberras. One aircraft was subsequently modified to carry a custom-made radome as part of later research flying, and both remained active until 1973. *(Photo: Tim McLelland collection)*

Six Canberra B.Mk.6s were manufactured for France, although they were not destined for the French Air Force. They were assigned to test establishments (CEV and CTB) and used on research programmes, acting as a radar and engine test beds, and flying laboratories. One aircraft was subsequently modified with a B(I).Mk.8 forward fuselage. As with most trials aircraft, a great deal of research performed by these Canberras has not been publicised.
(Photo: David Ilot)

India began negotiations to acquire the Canberra as a replacement for its obsolete Consolidated B-24 Liberator bombers in 1954. In January 1957 it ordered 54 B(I).Mk.58 bombers, eight PR.Mk.57 reconnaissance aircraft and six T.Mk.4 trainers. Twelve more Canberras were ordered in September 1957, and another 30 had been purchased by 1962. The fleet was mostly grounded following the crash of an IAF Canberra in December 2005, although a small number of aircraft remained active on second-line duties. The Canberra was finally retired on 11 May 2007, after 50 years of Indian service. *(Photos: Tim McLelland collection)*

Martin B.57A Canberra 52-1418, 1953. This was the first production aircraft manufactured by Martin. Overall finish is unpainted metal (unlike RAF machines that were all sprayed silver). National insignia in standard positions with serials and titles in black.

Martin B-57B 52-1567. 405th Tactical Fighter Wing (8th TBS), 1969. Standard South East Asia camouflage comprising of Green (FS.34102), Green (FS.34079) and Tan (FS.30219) with black undersides. Codes are applied in black and white with full colour national insignia.

Canberra B.Mk.62 B-110, formerly RAF B.Mk.2 WJ619. Fuerza Aerea Argentina 1972. Standard RAF camouflage colours (Dark Sea Grey and Dark Green with Light Aircraft Grey undersides) with Argentine insignia in blue and white. Codes and titling in white.

Canberra TT.Mk.418 Q1791, Indian Air Force 2006. Formerly RAF Canberra T.Mk.4 WE193, the aircraft is painted in medium green colours with high visibility black and yellow undersides, combined with fluorescent orange trim.

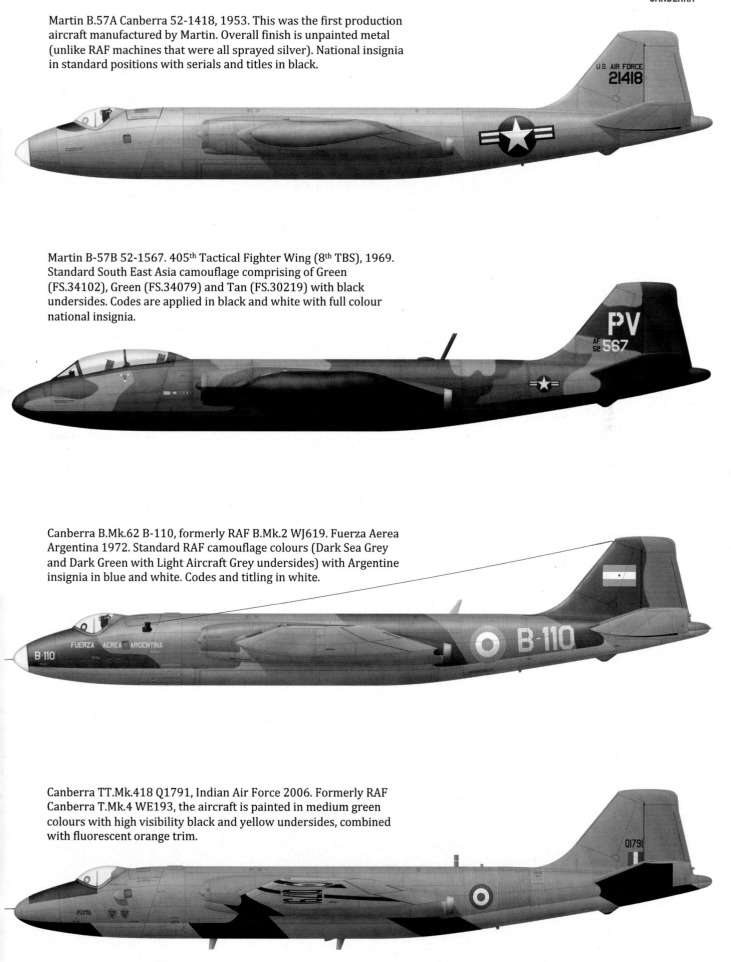

Drawings by Chris Sandham-Bailey (www.inkworm.co.uk)

Canberra B.Mk.2 WK163 effectively became a B.Mk.6 in 1968, when it was fitted with the wings and engines of a redundant Mk.6. After its withdrawal from MoD(PE) test flying, the aircraft joined the civil register and eventually became part of the Classic Air Force fleet at Coventry. It had been expected to return to airworthiness in 2015 but, now owned by the Vulcan to the Sky Trust, remained grounded early in 2024.
(Photo: Classic Air Force)

Following the end of XH134's operation, no British-built Canberra was airworthy anywhere in the world until 2021, when former RAF TT18 WJ680 flew again at Temora, New South Wales, as part of the Royal Australian Air Force's 100 Squadron — the service's historic flight, established to mark its centenary year. This aircraft had been acquired from its previous British owner by the Temora Aviation Museum in May 2001, and thereafter ferried to Australia. It was repainted to represent the Canberra bombers flown by the RAAF's 2 Squadron during the Vietnam conflict. Grounded in 2010, before its return to flight WJ680 underwent three years of work, including conversion of the Avon engines from the original explosive cartridge starters to electric starters. The Canberra was reflown on 28 June 2021.

Ex-No 39 (1 PRU) Squadron Canberra PR9 XH134 was restored to airworthiness for the Cotswold Airport-based Midair Squadron, flying again under civil registration G-OMHD in July 2013. Repainted in a silver scheme, the aircraft appeared on the airshow circuit late in the 2013 season, and made many appearances in 2014, such as here at the Jersey International Air Display. However, in the run-up to 2015's air displays, the operator went under, and XH134 has been grounded at Cotswold Airport ever since. *(Photo: Ben Dunnell)*